Time
Management

Ros Jay

- Fast track route to mastering all aspects of time management

- Covers all the key techniques for managing your time successfully, from clearing your desk to prioritization, and from good delegation to knowing how and when to say 'no'

- Examples and lessons from some of the world's most successful time managers, and ideas from the smartest thinkers, including Robert Paterson, Don Aslett and Stephen Covey

- Includes a glossary of key concepts and a comprehensive resources guide

LIFE & WORK

10.09

essential management thinking at your fingertips

First published 2002 by
Capstone Publishing (a Wiley company)
8 Newtec Place
Magdalen Road
Oxford OX4 1RE
United Kingdom
http://www.capstoneideas.com

CIP catalogue records for this book are available from the British Library and the US Library of Congress

ISBN 1-84112-254-8

Printed and bound in Great Britain

This book is printed on acid-free paper

Substantial discounts on bulk quantities of Capstone books are available to corporations, professional associations and other organizations. Please contact Capstone for more details on +44 (0)1865 798 623 or (fax) +44 (0)1865 240 941 or (e-mail) info@wiley-capstone.co.uk

Contents

Introduction to ExpressExec

ExpressExec is 3 million words of the latest management thinking compiled into 10 modules. Each module contains 10 individual titles forming a comprehensive resource of current business practice written by leading practitioners in their field. From brand management to balanced scorecard, ExpressExec enables you to grasp the key concepts behind each subject and implement the theory immediately. Each of the 100 titles is available in print and electronic formats.

Through the ExpressExec.com Website you will discover that you can access the complete resource in a number of ways:

» printed books or e-books;
» e-content – PDF or XML (for licensed syndication) adding value to an intranet or Internet site;
» a corporate e-learning/knowledge management solution providing a cost-effective platform for developing skills and sharing knowledge within an organization;
» bespoke delivery – tailored solutions to solve your need.

Why not visit www.expressexec.com and register for free key management briefings, a monthly newsletter and interactive skills checklists. Share your ideas about ExpressExec and your thoughts about business today.

Please contact elound@wiley-capstone.co.uk for more information.

Introduction to Time Management

Introduction to the discipline of time management

"It's not enough to be busy. The question is: what are we busy about?"

Henry David Thoreau

Time is the most valuable finite resource we have. When we first start work, fresh out of school or college, we generally find ourselves at the bottom of the heap. Our time is largely allocated for us. We're told to complete this or that task, and then move on to the next item on the list we're given. We don't have to think about how we organize our time, because we *don't* organize it; someone else does. The process actually begins at school, and by the time we enter the world of work it's already ingrained in us.

As we move up the organization into more senior posts, we gradually acquire more control over our own time. As our authority to choose tasks and to make decisions increases, so does our authority to organize our own time. But it creeps up on us gradually, and we often slip into habits that may be holding us back – without our realization.

Some workers are given training in time management at some stage. It's usually only a day or two, at the most, and it's rarely renewed; the memory of it usually fades quickly into the distant past. Many workers never receive any training at all. The skill of time management is one that many managers have to learn ad hoc. Some have a fairly good natural bent in that direction, while others haven't a clue what it's all about – or how anyone is supposed to find the time to practice good time management. Yet, time management skills are essential to any successful manager. You'd be hard pressed to find anyone who has reached the top of the career ladder without having learnt how to make the best and most effective use of their time.

This book explains what time management is all about, and why it is so important – especially at managerial level. We'll be covering the following issues and topics.

» What precisely is time management?
» How has the need to manage time evolved and increased?
» How can we cope with the additional demands on our time posed by the arrival of the computer and the Internet?
» Key time management techniques that senior executives need to use.

» The latest time management tools and aids, and the way in which new styles of work will have an impact on time management over the next few years.
» Case studies, to show how managers have incorporated key time management skills into their work, in order to become more effective.
» What are the most important ideas and who are the significant people in the world of time management?
» A guide to the most important resources available – books, organizations and websites – to expand your knowledge and skills.
» A summary of the most important practical time management skills that will ensure you get the most value from your time.

Managers who have mastered time management stand out a mile for being able to achieve more in every day than most other managers achieve in a week. And the most effective also get to spend their evenings and weekends with their family and friends, rather than being stuck in the office trying to clear the backlog of work. (Backlogs are for people who can't manage their time.)

Managing time at work is becoming increasingly difficult, as rising expectations and new technology place extra demands on workers. It is essential to keep abreast of time management skills, and to recognize the latest trends and new developments in the field, in order to achieve maximum effectiveness in those 24 hours a day.

What is Time Management?

"It is those who make the worst use of their time who most complain of its shortness."

Jean de la Bruyere

If you sit and twiddley our thumbs all day, time will still pass. What's more, it will pass at the same speed for you as it will for everyone else (even if it doesn't seem like it). Unlike most resources – money, equipment, and so on – time is fixed. You cannot possibly create any more of it. If the work you do doesn't fit into the time you have, the work is the only thing you can change. And that's what time management is all about.

There are numerous ways of adapting the work – of fitting what appears to be too much work into too little time – but in essence there are two key approaches:

» reduce the amount of work; and
» get through the same amount of work more effectively.

These two methods are at the heart of time management. Time management is also concerned with making sure that, when you do fit your work into the available time, it is the *right work*. The most valuable work you can do is the work that helps you meet your core objectives.

REDUCE THE AMOUNT OF WORK

If you cannot fit all your work into the time you have, the most obvious recourse is probably to reduce the amount of work you have. Many busy people, from juniors to CEOs, find it hard to see how this can be done. In fact, there are almost always ways that executives can cut down on their work. Time management techniques advocate slimming down the workload in several ways.

» *Dump unnecessary work*. Most of us engage in tasks that simply are not necessary, such as reading papers and journals that don't really add anything to our performance, or double-checking departmental time sheets when the supervisor can do it perfectly well without our back-up.
» *Delegate*. The art of delegation is a huge topic. It's a central part of time management, since effective delegation is a major time-saver.

» *Reduce time spent in meetings*. Most managers cite time spent in meetings as one of the worst time-wasters. That's not to say all meetings are a waste of time – in fact, they can represent the most effective use of time – but many of them are. The answer is to find ways of not being there if it's not going to help you get your job done.
» *Get it right first time*. Redoing work is a huge time-eater for many people. Good time management means making sure it's right from the start, which often entails insisting on a clear brief before starting.
» *Communicate effectively*. Good communication skills overlap with time management skills. Poor communication often leads to work being done incorrectly or taking longer than it should. Communicating well with your team also means that they can work more time-effectively too.

GET THROUGH THE SAME AMOUNT OF WORK MORE EFFECTIVELY

Working efficiently isn't enough – you also have to work *effectively*. Efficient workers get plenty done, but it may not be the most effective work they could do, or at the most effective time. Good time management demands that every task you do should be carried out effectively so that none of your hard work is wasted.

According to management guru Peter Drucker, the major problem is "fundamentally the confusion between effectiveness and efficiency that stands between doing the right things and doing things right. There is surely nothing quite so useless as doing with greater efficiency what should not be done at all."

» *Plan*. Work out schedules in advance, adopt thorough diary-keeping skills, and make to-do lists. This is one of the best-known aspects of time management.
» *Assess tasks and projects in advance*. Before you start a project or a major task, you need to know what you intend to achieve and how. Without this assessment you cannot plan effectively (and get your planning right first time). You have to know how long the task or project will take, what resources you will need, what standard

you need to achieve, and any other constraints, such as deadline or budget.

» *Organize*. You can achieve far more in the same amount of time if you are well organized. This means keeping on top of the filing, keeping your desk clear of clutter, and so on.

» *Be more productive*. Smart time managers are always looking for ways to speed up tasks. From learning speed-reading to taking advantage of the latest computer technology, there are always new methods of working faster.

» *Don't waste time*. The working day is full of little bits of wasted time – holding on the phone, waiting for the modem to connect, being kept waiting for appointments and meetings. Time management can be improved hugely by utilizing all these bits of time for planning projects, generating ideas, writing a quick e-mail or catching up on 30 seconds' filing.

» *Focus*. Doing one task at a time is far more effective that flitting from one thing to the next and back again. Use the simple expedient of diverting calls while you concentrate on writing a report; group together all the tasks relating to a major project instead of dotting them about through the day.

» *Know your own patterns*. Some people are more productive in the morning, while others do their best thinking in the evening, or straight after lunch. Learn to recognize your own optimum times for each type of task, and then work to your strengths.

» *Cut down interruptions*. You'll never manage your time effectively unless you can get other people to co-operate. Find ways to reduce interruptions – face-to-face or by phone – in order to work more effectively.

» *Make meetings more productive*. If you're in the chair, good time management techniques will enable you to make sure that every second of your meeting is time well spent.

» *Stop procrastinating*. From writer's block when it comes to an important proposal, to putting off drawing up next year's budget because you simply can't face it, procrastination is the enemy of good time management. There are plenty of techniques for making yourself knuckle down to those tedious or nerve-wracking tasks, along with those that are easier and more fun.

DO THE RIGHT WORK

It's all very well being familiar with these techniques, as long as you achieve what you're supposed to (as Peter Drucker pointed out). Despite working extremely hard, many managers never really make a significant positive impression on their organization. Time management concerns itself with this, too. It's not enough to work effectively; you have to be doing the *right* work. The further up the organization you move, the more important it is to get this aspect of time management right.

» *Create time for doing the right work*. Most of the really important achievements made by executives are pro-active or self-generated. If you merely react to problems as they crop up, you will not make your mark on the job. When are you going to find the time to generate ideas and projects? Time management comes in here; you cannot call yourself a smart time manager unless you know how to create time for pro-active tasks.

» *Define your objectives*. What pro-active tasks should you work on in the time you generate? Again, you need to be effective, and you cannot do that unless you know precisely what your objectives are.

» *Set goals*. Your objectives are your overall strategy, but in order to be able to see clearly where you're headed, you have to put those objectives into the form of clear goals. Only then can you plan your time, knowing precisely what you intend to achieve, and when.

» *Determine your priorities*. If you have a long list of tasks you need to achieve, and you can't do them all at once, where do you start? This question is key to time management. Much of time management is about setting priorities, and identifying those tasks that are important, as distinct from those that are urgent.

» *Measure your progress*. If you don't know how well you're doing, how can you tell whether your time management techniques are working? In short, you can't. It's important to monitor everything you do in order to establish how effective it is.

All the techniques of the discipline of time management are, of course, integrated. You can only achieve excellence in time management if *everything* you do is effective. You cannot plan effectively unless you have determined your objectives and set your goals, and you cannot carry out your plan effectively without good time management techniques.

Top executives who have really got time management sorted can run multinational organizations without ever staying late at the office or working all weekend. This aspect of time management is increasingly being recognized as important for everyone: good time management applies at home as well as at work. It is only when you are a high achiever at work and you have time for a full life away from work too that you can truly call yourself a master of time management.

KEY LEARNING POINTS

Better time management can be achieved through three approaches to work.

» Reduce the amount of work.
» Get through the same amount of work more effectively.
» Do the right work.

Reduce the amount of work

» Dump unnecessary work.
» Delegate.
» Reduce time spent in meetings.
» Get it right first time.
» Communicate effectively.

Get through the same amount of work more effectively

» Plan.
» Assess tasks and projects in advance.
» Organize.
» Be more productive.
» Don't waste time.
» Focus.
» Know your own patterns.
» Cut down interruptions.
» Make meetings more productive.
» Stop procrastinating.

Do the right work

- » Create time for doing the right work.
- » Define your objectives.
- » Set goals.
- » Determine your priorities.
- » Measure your progress.

10.09.03

Evolution of Time Management

"Our costliest expenditure is time."

Theophrastus (370–287 BC), Greek philosopher

According to anthropologists, Stone Age hunter-gatherers could survive comfortably on a working week of just 15 hours. But it was only a matter of time before people discovered that a greater input of time could bring greater rewards. As civilization progressed, so the length of the working week increased. It took more hours to survive as a farmer than as a hunter – all that working the soil and sowing and harvesting – but it paid dividends in the form of a more static and comfortable lifestyle.

The earliest references to time management come from the Benedictine monks, who were making a point of scheduling their activities from at least the sixth century AD. As communities became more structured and organized, so a form of time management inevitably crept in. However, for many centuries, although time was allocated and scheduled, no study was made of how to maximize time as a valuable resource.

Apart from anything else, it's quite difficult to be very precise about use of time when there is no accurate way of measuring it. In the past, people referred to time in terms of natural events: dawn, "when the sun is overhead", dusk, and so on. Until the fourteenth century there were no clocks in regular use, and it wasn't until the late seventeenth century that the technology was developed to make reliable timepieces. Use of clocks did not become widespread until the eighteenth century.

ADAM SMITH

By the early 1700s, factory owners were beginning to impose more time discipline on their workers. Many factories introduced some form of timesheet, and imposed fines on workers who arrived late. In England, Josiah Wedgwood (1730–95) introduced the first-ever system of clocking-in at his Staffordshire potteries.

In the mean time, economist Adam Smith was developing his theories, expounded in *An Inquiry into the Nature and Causes of the Wealth of Nations*. This theoretical treatise on capitalism argued that the amount of labor in a product determines its value; in other words, a nation's wealth is generated by the time spent working. Modern-day economists no longer agree with his view.

Smith went on to argue that greater efficiency would lead to the creation of greater wealth, and that saving time – both for management and workers – was a direct factor in profitability. He advocated division of labor, both between factories and within them, in order to maximize efficiency.

BENJAMIN FRANKLIN

Often regarded as the father of time management – and certainly of personal time management – Benjamin Franklin was a contemporary of Adam Smith. This extraordinary man, an inventor, publisher, philosopher, diplomat and American statesman, started his business life very shakily. At the age of 28, he found himself penniless and jobless, having twice filed for bankruptcy.

Franklin's solution to his problems was to change his approach to work. He taught himself to set goals and to prioritize, and he kept a little black book (today it would be called a daily planner), where he recorded his activities. He aimed to live up to a set of 13 basic values – from humility to frugality – and made notes in his book each evening, reporting on his daily performance in respect of these values.

Franklin became a high-profile writer and a deeply respected man, and many of his views were accepted readily. He wrote much on the subject of managing time, asking the important question, "Dost thou love life? Then do not squander time, for that is the stuff life is made of." His work also happened to coincide with a growth in industrialization, and an increasing belief in a completely new concept – "Time is money" – a phrase coined by Franklin himself.

Franklin's approach might be summed up by one of his most pertinent pieces of writing.

"If you want to enjoy one of the greatest luxuries in life, the luxury of having enough time, time to rest, time to think things through, time to get things done and know you have done them to the best of your ability, remember there is only one way. Take enough time to think and plan things in the order of their importance. Your life will take on a new zest, you will add years to your life, and more life to your years. Let all your things have their places.''

ELI WHITNEY

American inventor Eli Whitney may have been most famous for his ''cotton gin'', which separated cotton from seeds, but, in terms of time management, his most significant invention had nothing to do with cotton.

Whitney's cotton gin was so valuable that it was frequently pirated and, eventually, Congress refused to renew its patent. As a result, Whitney went out of business. Disgusted with his experiences in the cotton-growing southern states, he decided to move north, to find a profitable line of business that might enable him to pay off his debts.

He decided that the US government would be his most likely investor, and he looked for an idea that it might want to bankroll. In 1798, the United States was preparing for war with France, but one of the government's greatest problems was that it didn't have enough muskets. The process of making them – which could only be done by skilled gunsmiths – was painfully slow. In three years, the government had stockpiled barely a thousand. Whitney told the government that he could make 10,000 muskets in just two and a half years, including allowing time to set up the factory. The government jumped at the offer.

Whitney subscribed to Adam Smith's principle of increasing efficiency. His idea was to use machines rather than men to make the weapons. That way, he could generate identical and replaceable parts, any of which would fit any musket, instead of being unique and custom-made for one musket only. This ''uniformity system'' meant that unskilled laborers could operate the machines, and skilled gunsmiths were not required to produce the weapons. It was the start of mass production.

In fact, problems with buying the factory site, and hold-ups due to severe weather and an epidemic of yellow fever, meant that Whitney missed his deadline. But he had made his point. His ideas of mass production revolutionized the northern states, creating an industrial boom, and providing jobs for thousands of unskilled workers.

Whitney's activities meant that Adam Smith's ideas of increased efficiency and division of labor were advanced further than he could ever have imagined. It became clear that it was possible to manufacture products in a fraction of the time, and that machines were capable of far greater levels of efficiency than people.

THE NINETEENTH AND EARLY TWENTIETH CENTURY

Nineteenth-century factory owners were increasingly concerned with time, which they now recognized as equalling money. Until now, ordinary people had not concerned themselves with such details. Clocks may have been around for 150 years, but most workers didn't have them in their houses, let alone carry them around. Timekeeping was still a very relaxed business.

But that wasn't the way the business owners wanted it. They wanted to get the maximum input from their workers in order to achieve the maximum output from their factories. And because the machinery needed many people to operate it, they all had to be there at the same time. As community historian Carl Chinn puts it, "What the gaffers did, they brought in fines, they tried to force the working people into this concept of time that was very much alien to so many of us and over the century there was lots of tension. You can see that in the rules and regulations of mill owners and factory owners trying to force their workers to clock in and clock off at a regular time."

The Pareto Principle

At the very end of the nineteenth century, Italian economist Vilfredo Pareto noted that 80 per cent of the land in England was owned by 20 per cent of the population. He studied the balance further, and discovered that it applied to every other country he looked at. He then went on to find that the 80/20 "predictable imbalance" also applied to other aspects of life.

Many economists since Pareto have expanded upon this theory, which became known as the Pareto Principle. It is the basis of one central theory of time management, which states that 20 per cent of the time put into work generates 80 per cent of the results. Identifying our most effective 20 per cent, and extending it, can have a huge positive impact on our productivity.

Work study

At the same time as Pareto was forming his 80/20 principle, many other engineers and scientists were looking for ways to get more work done in the same amount of time. At the turn of the twentieth century, when many business owners were looking for ways to increase productivity, *work study* became popular. The idea of scientific management was born.

The concept was created by Frederick W. Taylor, who advocated the observation and measuring of the activities of workers, in order to hone and streamline production systems. Taylor believed that all workers were motivated solely by money, and recommended incentive payments to boost performance and productivity. In his view, "Hardly a competent workman can be found who does not devote a considerable amount of time to studying just how slowly he can work and still convince his employer that he is going at a good pace."

Many of Taylor's ideas have subsequently been discredited, such as his views on motivation, and his calls for a standardized production line (very efficient, but limiting in terms of customer choice). Nevertheless, his ideas represented a great leap forward at the time, and provided the groundwork for the later principles of measuring effectiveness and getting the most work out of the least time.

Frank and Lilian Gilbreth also applied work study techniques, setting up the Human Betterment Lab in Rhode Island. They carried out various odd experiments, such as attaching light bulbs to workers' fingers so that they could trace the patterns of their movements and work out the most efficient way to do any task. (Something of an obsessive, Frank Gilbreth even taught his 12 children the most efficient way of having a bath.)

One of F.W. Taylor's advocates was Henry Ford, who adopted Taylor's techniques and applied them to his methods of mass production. Ford was a keen proponent of time management: "It has been my observation that most people get ahead during the time that others waste."

STEPHEN R. COVEY

By the 1950s, the emphasis of time management was starting to shift towards incorporating the individual manager's skills at organizing personal time – back to where Benjamin Franklin had come in. The first book on time management appeared in the late 1950s, and since then the discipline has evolved considerably.

To begin with, "time management" was mostly concerned with learning how to make notes and keep reminders. Later proponents of the discipline recommended ways to plan and prepare, using calendars and better diary skills. Today, time management covers a wider range of issues, including goal-setting, prioritizing and controlling.

The most successful time management guru of them all is Stephen R. Covey, whose book, *The 7 Habits of Highly Effective People* (Simon & Schuster, 1989), has sold over 12 million copies in over 30 languages. It is a self-awareness guide that aims to help people become more effective, more sensitive and more confident. While not concentrating exclusively on time management, the discipline is nevertheless a key aspect of the book. *Fortune* Magazine has described Covey as one of the 25 most influential Americans.

In 1997, Covey's organization, the Covey Leadership Center, merged with Franklin Quest, led by Hyrum W. Smith, to form Franklin Covey – one of the biggest businesses in time management. The consultancy offers training and seminars, and also sells millions of Franklin planners, which get their name from one of the original time management gurus, Benjamin Franklin.

According to Hyrum W. Smith, "We're not in the planner business, we're not even in the seminar business, we're in the personal control business. As long as there's anyone on the planet who's out of control, there's a market for what we do. You think our marketplace will ever evaporate?"

KEY DATES IN THE EVOLUTION OF TIME MANAGEMENT

» Benedictine monks: Sixth century AD
» Invention of accurate clocks: 1674

» Adam Smith: 1723–90
» Benjamin Franklin: 1706–90
» Eli Whitney: 1765–1825
» Frederick W. Taylor: 1856–1917
» Stephen R. Covey: 1932–

KEY LEARNING POINTS

» *Pre-eighteenth century*: no accurate means of measuring time.
» *Adam Smith: Wealth of Nations* emphasized the importance of saving time and making greater efficiencies, especially through division of labor.
» *Benjamin Franklin*: pioneered personal time management, including goal-setting and prioritizing.
» *Eli Whitney*: invented mass production with his "uniformity system" of identical and replaceable parts.
» *Nineteenth and early twentieth century*: workers gradually forced to accept more accurate timekeeping; Pareto Principle; Frederick W. Taylor introduces the concept of scientific management, and uses work study to measure and improve workers' efficiency.
» *Stephen R. Covey*: from the 1950s, personal time management is recognized as an important discipline. By the 1980s and 90s, Stephen R. Covey and other key time management thinkers are advocating using time management for everything from keeping notes to setting goals.

The E-Dimension

"Imagine if every Thursday your shoes exploded if you tied them the usual way. This happens to us all the time with computers, and nobody thinks of complaining."

Jeff Raskin

The arrival of the Internet and electronic mail has had a significant impact on time management. Many of the innovations they have brought have been extremely beneficial (see Chapter 6), but they also have a nasty habit of eating up time. From e-mailing to Net surfing, new technology has put even more demands on our time. If we want to avoid spending too much time online, we need to adopt new techniques.

E-MAIL

E-mail has done wonders for time management. You can now communicate with other people in minutes instead of days, even if they're on the other side of the globe. And not only do e-mails travel faster than snail mail, they have also developed their own, far briefer style. You can send a one-word e-mail – you'd never do that with a letter. At the other extreme, you can send large amounts of information fast, without the drawbacks of faxing, such as possible delays and the need to copy or re-key material.

But for all the undoubted benefits in terms of saving time, many people complain that e-mail technology can also *waste* time. E-mails provide yet another interruption or distraction. The mail all turns up at once; you have to answer many of them, and you have to read a lot of the others, only to discover that they're junk. There's no doubt that your list of tasks is longer than it was before the days of e-mail. Some people spend literally hours a day dealing with e-mails; that's hardly an improvement in time management.

In order to get the best from this new technology, you have to find ways of controlling your e-mails before they control you. You need to make the time you spend dealing with them – incoming and outgoing – as brief as possible, so you can really reap the benefits of the technology without suffering the disadvantages.

Dealing with incoming e-mail

» Don't pick up your e-mail every few minutes, or allow an incoming message to interrupt you. Only check your e-mail when you have time to deal with it, and schedule specific times to check it. These might be first thing in the morning, after lunch (if you have time), and late afternoon, about 4.30ish – that still gives you time to reply to anything urgent before people go home for the day.

» Set your software to pick up e-mails automatically. Unless you expect urgent e-mails, every hour or two is plenty. This means that, at the allotted times when you come to deal with your e-mails, they will be waiting for you; you won't have to wait to log on before collecting them.

» Program your software to hang up when it has finished picking up e-mails.

» If you check for e-mails other than automatically, try to do it at off-peak times, when it is much quicker. The Internet is increasingly slow during peak times, as it gets busier.

» Sort your incoming e-mail so you can deal with related documents all at once, instead of interrupting your flow by jumping from one subject to another and back again. You can sort by author, for example, or by subject or keyword.

» Since you are now picking up your e-mails at scheduled times, you can deal with them immediately. Reply to all the messages you can straight away; you'll just waste time if you keep rereading them until you get round to it.

» If an e-mail doesn't need a reply, don't reply to it.

» Don't print out e-mails unless you really need to. You may need the document on file, an attachment printed out to read on the train going home, or a copy to take into a meeting. Otherwise, leave it on the screen where it belongs or, better still, delete it.

» Be ruthless about removing yourself from any mailing list you don't need to be on. E-mail a reply to the sender with the word "Unsub-scribe" in the subject line. Organizations that want to sell you things can always mail a hard copy of the information to you instead. It may take a couple of days longer, but why should you care?

» If you can see from the sender or the headline that the e-mail is either junk or simply not relevant to you, don't even read it. Just delete it.

» Don't allow friends and colleagues to send you endless funny stories, latest jokes and urban myths. E-mail them to let them know that your computer is a work tool and you don't have time to read any e-mails that are not work-related.

Speeding up outgoing e-mail

» Schedule times to send e-mails all at once, preferably immediately after picking up your latest e-mails. Don't keep interrupting other work to send them.

» Have a tray in which to keep paperwork and notes about e-mails you plan to send. Then when you have an e-mail session you know where to find whatever you need.

» In order to speed things up for other people as well as yourself, always put a suitable title in the subject field. This will also help you if they reply.

» If you need an urgent reply, say so in the subject line (for example, "Please reply by Tuesday evening").

» Many people won't have time to read your e-mail thoroughly, so put the most important information or questions in the first paragraph.

» If you have several things to say, put them in a bullet-pointed list.

» You can use the "Urgent message" notation to draw the recipient's attention to your message. But if it isn't really urgent, or you use it too often, your recipients will no longer believe you – and may not read your message properly.

» Don't copy e-mails to people who don't need them.

» If you send attachments, make sure the person receiving them will be able to read them. Otherwise you could waste your time and theirs trying to sort out the problem later.

» If you are attaching a large file, zip it so that you can send it faster. Zip software compresses the file and the recipient simply unzips it to read it. For a free trial download of the Windows version, visit www.winzip.com.

» Use cut and paste when you can to speed up composing e-mails. You can use this if you send a similar e-mail to several people, or if you want to repeat part of the sender's message back.

» Keep e-mails concise.
» Learn some basic e-mail shorthand. There are plenty of phrases and symbols in common use to speed up writing e-mails. Learn to read them and use them to save time. Here are a few of the most popular: BTW, by the way; FAQ, frequently asked questions; FWIW, for what it's worth; FYI, for your information; IOW, in other words; OTOH, on the other hand; TIA, thanks in advance; TNX, thanks; :-) pleased; :-(sad; :-/ confused. There are plenty more, but you'll need to be sure that your correspondent is able to interpret them. You can find them easily online, ask friends and colleagues, or buy a small guide.

Organizing your e-mail archive

» Don't keep e-mails you don't need.
» If you do keep e-mails, don't store them all in your Inbox, Sent items or Deleted items folders. File them in appropriate subject folders so you can find them quickly and easily when you need them.
» Take back-up copies of anything essential.
» Keep your e-mail address book up to date, and use it to store contact addresses, phone numbers and so on, too.

Remember your e-mail etiquette

» E-mail won't do for everything. If diplomacy is called for, or detailed negotiation, it is far more effective to speak to someone directly than to e-mail them.
» Likewise, any kind of negative or bad news message is best delivered personally.
» When we write a letter we tend to think carefully about how we word it. Half the point of e-mail is that we can write as we speak and save ourselves that time we might otherwise have spent chewing the end of our pencil. However, the risk is that we will write something in all innocence that reads to the recipient as brusque, sarcastic or even downright rude. If there's any chance of this, reread your e-mail before you send it to make sure it sounds as you intend. If there's a danger something might be taken the wrong way, use the smile symbol :-) to indicate that you don't intend any offence.
» Never send anything confidential by e-mail.
» Don't send non-work-related messages to the work address of a friend or colleague without their express agreement.

THE INTERNET

The Net has taken days off the time it can take to do research or to contact an organization and get information from it. The trouble is, when people go online, many seem to enter a time warp. Everything you're doing is relevant and useful, but you suddenly find you've been logged on for *two hours*; you never meant to devote that much time to whatever it is you're doing.

Like e-mailing, using the Net seems to waste as much time as it saves. You need to find ways to avoid wasting time so that you gain all the advantages of the technology without incurring the disadvantages. Here are the top ideas for doing just that.

Finding a website fast

» You don't necessarily have to type the whole URL (website address) to locate a website. You can usually skip the http:// at the front. In Navigator 2.0 or later you can also leave off the "www" prefix and omit the suffix ".com". If the address has some other prefix or suffix, however, you will have to enter it.

» If you don't have the URL of an organization's website, just try the company name (all as one word) with the prefix www. Add the suffix .com or anything else you think is likely (such as .co.uk, .au, or whatever). This may get you straight there. If not, you can always use a search engine to look for it.

» Many web pages have very long addresses with plenty of forward slashes to get you to the exact page. If you have trouble logging on to these, just delete everything after the .com (or whatever suffix is used) to get back to the home page.

» If you get fed up waiting for a page with complex graphics to download, you can always speed it up by downloading the text only. Wait until the page starts to appear, then press ⟨Esc⟩ to download words without pictures.

» Just because the Internet is there, you don't have to use it. If you want, for example, a quick piece of information, such as a product price, from an organization whose URL you don't have, it's probably quicker to phone the company's main switchboard than to try to track it down online.

Fast searches

» To choose your own home page (the one that opens up first every time you go online), go to "Options" in your browser and select a page that is useful to you. If you frequently use the Internet to do searches, set your favorite search engine as your home page.

» Use bookmarks to identify favorite and frequently visited sites, so that you can find them again quickly. Delete any bookmarks that you haven't used for a while so that your list doesn't become too long and unwieldy.

» Don't stick to one favorite search engine. Get to know at least four or five, and use the most suitable. Some are better for worldwide searches, while others are more appropriate for a national search. They all have different keywords, search speeds, and so on; different engines are fastest for different searches.

» Learn how to use search terms to best effect. If you enter time management as two words, you'll be offered all the sites with *either* the word "time" *or* the word "management." To ask the search engine to look for the phrase as a whole, put it into quotation marks: "time management". The search engine will only come up with sites and pages that contain the whole phrase of "time management".

» Speed up searches by using more keywords. The number of time management sites is huge, but if you add the word "travel," you can limit the sites you are offered to those that are about *both* time management *and* travel. Tell the search engine you want to look for the overlap between these two topics by inserting a plus sign between the two: "time management" + travel.

» You can do much the same thing in reverse by inserting a minus sign. If you want to know about time management, but don't want to be plagued by travel tips, ask the search engine to look for time management sites, but *not* those that deal with travel: "time management" – travel.

» If you want variations on a word, you can use what are known as wildcards, usually * (your search engine will tell you what symbol to use). Entering "time manag*" will produce sites that refer to time management, time managing, time managers and so on.

» If you are using a search engine and want to open several windows, you don't have to wait for each one to download. Instead of left-clicking on the mouse, use the right-click button to open up a different menu. From this, select "Open in new window." As soon as the window appears, minimize it and carry on looking through the search engine listing. When you're ready, click on the bar at the bottom of the screen to open each downloaded window in turn.

Speeding things up

» If your Internet connection is slow, upgrade to a faster connection if you can. There are many high-speed Internet connections on the market, and they will save you a lot of downloading time.

» The more fragmented your computer storage becomes, the slower it gets. When you create a new file, your computer allocates it storage space. Once it outgrows this space, the operating system splits the file so it can store it in more than one space. So it takes longer to retrieve information, open files and so on. The answer is to defragment your hard drive; this simple process organizes information more efficiently and speeds up your computer. (If you are using Windows, you can do this by following the route Start/Programs/Accessories/System Tools/Disk defragmenter.) The more often you defragment, the quicker the process; aim to do it once a week, when you're not using the computer for anything else. Set it up to defragment as you start making phone calls, for example, or as you head off to a meeting. If you leave it for several months, it will take a few hours to defragment.

» Install a good software package to protect you from viruses. Be aware that you are vulnerable to viruses if you ever download files from websites, use e-mails or generally use the Internet.

» Delete automatic back-up files. They occupy valuable space on your hard disk and slow things down.

» Set the "Autosave" function to save files as often as you want. If you set it to save every five minutes, you won't lose more than the last five minutes of work if there's a power failure or your computer crashes.

» Back up all your work on to floppy or other removable disks. If you don't back up at the end of each day it's only a matter of time before you regret it. As they say, "The world of computers is divided into two types of people: those who have had a hard disk crash, and those who are going to."

E-mail and the Internet can be two of the greatest time-savers around, or two of the greatest time-wasters, depending on how you use them. It's up to you.

KEY LEARNING POINTS

E-mail
» Deal with incoming e-mail swiftly.
» Speed up outgoing e-mail.
» Organize your e-mail archive.
» Remember e-mail etiquette.

The Internet
» Find websites fast.
» Learn to do fast searches.
» Speed up your computer systems.

Time Management for Executives

» Goal-setting
  » Identifying goals
  » Achieving your goals
» Traveling time
» Dealing with deadlines
» Spending less time in meetings
  » Meetings you chair
  » Meetings chaired by others
» Key learning points

"The pursuit of excellence is gratifying and healthy; the pursuit of perfection is frustrating, neurotic, and a terrible waste of time."

Anonymous

The more senior you are, the more important it is to be able to manage your time. No one else is going to do it for you and strong time management skills will make you a far more effective and successful manager. As you rise up the organization, different and new issues of time management will evolve. Running streamlined meetings or making effective decisions didn't come into it when you were in a junior position. As you gain seniority, however, they become essential to your personal time flow, your effectiveness and your reputation.

This chapter covers the key skills you need to be able to manage your time when involved in senior management tasks. The more your time is occupied by such tasks, the greater the potential for time-saving as a result of putting these skills into action.

GOAL-SETTING

When you start at the bottom of an organization, you're told what you have to achieve: "Keep on top of the filing," "Sell this to anyone who phones in to place an order," "Package up everything on the list, and get it ready to send out by 5pm."

As you move on up, however, the boundaries you are set are much looser. In order to achieve the most you can, you need to start setting your own targets. The further you rise, the more autonomy you have and the more vital goal-setting becomes.

Goal-setting is an important part of time management because it ensures that you spend your time doing the right things. Without clear goals, it's possible to achieve a huge amount that doesn't need to be achieved, and doesn't really benefit the organization – it's a waste of time, in other words. Clear goals will keep you on track, helping you to focus on the most productive, effective and beneficial tasks, and ensuring that not a minute of your time is wasted.

Identifying goals

Of course, if you want to achieve the most that you can, you have to set the *right* goals. What are they? Primarily, they should reflect as closely as possible your real purpose in the organization. If you are responsible for sales, for example, any goal relating to an increase in sales is going to be appropriate.

Subsequently, you need to identify *key* goals. Equipping your entire sales team with better-quality company cars may make you popular, but it won't affect the bottom line. That's not to say that you mustn't do it, but it shouldn't be a key goal and therefore shouldn't occupy the majority of your time.

Identifying goals in key areas will help everyone to further their objectives.

» Work – your goal might be to reduce staff turnover by 20 per cent, or to increase your profit margin by 3 per cent.
» Personal – your goal might be to achieve a raise by the end of the year, or to learn another language.
» Home – especially if you have a family, it's worth setting goals in this area too. For example, you could aim to be home in time to read your children a bedtime story at least three nights a week, or to go away with your partner for a weekend every two months.

Write down your goals in your planner or diary, so that you feel more committed to them, and so that you can go back later and see whether you have achieved them yet, or how far you have to go.

Achieving your goals

You'll soon lose heart if your goals are unachievable, or if you can't tell whether you've achieved them, or whether you are close to achieving them. As you write down each goal, make sure that it

» is in line with your overall objectives;
» is clear;
» is measurable;
» is challenging but achievable; and
» has a deadline.

Now you know how you should be spending the bulk of your time. As you achieve each goal, set another one, to keep yourself moving towards your overall objectives. In order to make your goal-setting really effective, you'll find the following guidelines helpful.

» Several short-term goals are easier to achieve than a few long term ones. Instead of aiming to reduce complaints by four per cent in a year, consider aiming to reduce them by one per cent per quarter for the next year. Rather than aiming to read to your children three nights a week by two months from now, consider setting a target date by which you'll be consistently reading to them once a week; then set another date by which it will be twice a week; then set the two-month date by which you'll be up to three nights each week.

» Think hard about the timeframe you set for each goal. You'll quickly become disillusioned if you always miss the deadline – even if you eventually meet the goal. Be realistic. Don't set a deadline by which you'd *like* to achieve the goal; settle on a deadline by which you *can* achieve it. Keep it challenging, but remember it must also be achievable.

» To help you set a realistic timeframe, think through *how* you will achieve the goal. This should give you a good clue as to how long it will take. If the measures that will reduce staff turnover are going to take six months to establish, there's no point in setting a target of significantly reducing turnover in three months. At this stage you need only have an outline plan, but without that you cannot even know if your goal is achievable, let alone how long it will take.

» Scheduling time into your diary for working towards your goals is absolutely essential. You know that, if you don't block in time, you're hardly likely to have gaps when you sit at your desk, twiddling your thumbs, and think, "Hey! Now might be a good time to think about my goals." If you don't schedule in the time, *you will not achieve your goals*. Spend time early in the process on planning (this is why you need only an outline plan to set your timeframe), and then use the time to put your plans into action.

» The time you schedule must be inviolate. It's not "free" time, to allocate to other emergencies as they crop up. Spending time on your goals is the most important and effective thing you can do, and your goals are the last thing that should give in an emergency. Refusing to give up time scheduled for working towards goals is what marks out truly successful and effective managers and leaders from the rest.

TRAVELING TIME

Whether it's commuting by train, sitting in traffic jams or jetting around the world, traveling can take up a huge proportion of an executive's time – time that you really can't afford to waste. The more you can achieve at the same time as traveling, the less you will have to cram in once you reach your destination.

To begin with, choose the form of transport that suits you best. Some people find that driving gives them great thinking and planning time, while others find it hard to concentrate in the car. Train travel can be ideal if you have a lot of work that can be done on a laptop, or if you need to catch up on reading.

Long journeys are inevitably quicker by air, but on shorter hops it may be more productive to travel by train. A one-hour flight – complete with meal interruptions – can waste a lot of time. By the time you've got to the airport, allowed check-in time, and perhaps baggage reclaim, you've spent maybe three hours traveling with almost no work achieved. You might have spent perhaps three or four hours on the train, and used it all to get through a pile of work virtually undisturbed.

The trick is not to get stuck in a rut. Think about the best form of travel each time and adapt accordingly. You might commute by car one week and get lots of thinking time in, and switch to the train the following week to catch up on your reading. Choose the mode of transport according to the kind of work you can most usefully achieve while traveling.

Apart from this underlying principle, there are many more ways to make your traveling time more productive.

» Use time spent waiting (for trains, in traffic jams, collecting kids) to catch up on something useful – thinking and planning, or reading (carry a folder of reading material around with you).
» Keep a notebook with you when you're traveling, to jot down ideas and reminders.
» Listen to recorded books or language tapes in the car.
» If you are making a series of stops on your trip, arrange them as logically as you can to minimize traveling time.
» Write out a detailed itinerary, giving start and finish times of meetings as well as travel details and contact numbers at each place you'll be

visiting. Circulate this to each of the people you'll be meeting with so they recognize the need not to waste your time. Leave a copy with the office and another at home, too.

» Keep a list of frequently used phone numbers on you permanently – it can save you a lot of time when you're away from base.

» Keep in regular touch with the office to collect messages, and pick up your e-mails regularly when you're away. This will reduce the backlog of work when you return.

» If you regularly make overnight trips or longer, make a permanent packing list (filed on computer) of everything you need to take with you. You may need to divide it into things to pack from home and things to pack from the office. Each time you go away, just print off a clean list to work from, go through it, and tick off everything as you pack it. Add to your master list any time you need to.

» Keep a second set of toiletries – toothbrush, soap, flannel, and whatever else you need – permanently packed in addition to those you use at home. Instead of packing every item each time (and unpacking it when you get home), simply pick up the wash bag with everything already in it.

» If you travel with a laptop, make sure it's fully charged before you leave, and bring a fully charged spare battery too. And check that you have the extension leads and adaptors you might need to use and recharge it in your hotel room.

Don't forget that you are more productive when you are not over-worked (see *ExpressExec: Stress Management* and *ExpressExec: Body-care*). From time to time, the best thing you can do while you're traveling is sleep (one reason not to choose driving every time), or simply chill, meditate, or relax to music. It's OK to do this, too, when it seems the smartest option.

Time management is essentially about creating more time for your-self, not cramming every spare moment with extra work. The point about working while you travel is that it's more streamlined. It means that you should get to go home earlier, having achieved more.

DEALING WITH DEADLINES

Deadlines can be one of the most stressful and frustrating aspects of business life. As they approach, you become increasingly worried, you often find yourself working longer hours, and other work gets pushed aside. Even minor deadlines can play havoc with your time management. Consider the following measures to stop deadlines getting on top of you.

» Never agree to a deadline in the first place without thinking through whether it is realistic. If it isn't, simply explain that you can't meet it and offer an alternative – a more realistic date, or a phased delivery, with the first phase by the specified date and the remainder later.
» Break any major project down into smaller sections, and set yourself several mini-deadlines. This works for even a relatively small project, such as writing a report. Set a date by which you will complete your research, another for planning the report, another for drafting it, and another for completing it. This kind of scheduling makes your life easier, as each deadline is more manageable. However, you still have to recognize that it will work only if you adhere firmly to your schedule.
» If you can, always try to negotiate deadlines that are later than you need them to be. This means you have contingency time built in, in case unforeseen problems crop up (on this project or on something unrelated). When nothing does get in the way, you can impress everyone by completing the project early.

If you practice good time management skills in general, you will find that it is far easier to fit the work into the time allocated and meeting deadlines will be less of a problem.

SPENDING LESS TIME IN MEETINGS

Meetings you chair

You are responsible for the meetings you chair, and if they occupy more time than they warrant it is down to you. You can save loads of time by making your meetings more effective; you'll save not only your own time but also that of everyone else there.

» Do you need to hold the meeting at all? If not, don't. Could your weekly team meetings be fortnightly, for example? As Robert Heller has said, "A good sign that either the meeting or some of the people are superfluous is when they try to get out of coming."

» Avoid large meetings if possible; they're very time-consuming. Keep it small, perhaps by splitting it into two separate meetings. For example, ask a sub-group to meet and discuss certain key items that involve them, and then to send one representative to feed back to the main meeting.

» Make sure every item on the agenda has a purpose. It should be for information, action or decision – not for general waffling.

» Circulate an agenda that specifies what the outcome of every item will be – what decisions or actions will be taken, or what information will be imparted.

» The agenda should also state the start time for each item, and the finish time for the whole meeting.

» Circulate the agenda well in advance so that everyone has plenty of time to gather the information they need to bring with them.

» Insist that any background reading for any item be submitted to you in time to be circulated. Except in exceptional circumstances, don't allow paperwork to be circulated at the meeting that needs to be read immediately. It's very wasteful of time to have half a dozen people sitting in silence while they all read the same material that they could have been given a week before.

» Ban "Any Other Business" from your agendas. It gives people an excuse to bring up issues that others have not had a chance to prepare for. Quite apart from the Machiavellian opportunities this offers, it is a deeply ineffective way to tackle issues. People have to learn that any topic they want covered must be communicated to you *before* you write the agenda, unless it really is both last minute *and* too urgent to wait for the next meeting.

» Keep the meeting under control. Don't allow rabbitters to talk incessantly, bullies to dominate, or rivals to cause stand-up rows. Stay firmly in control by nipping any trouble in the bud, and never taking sides or showing favoritism.

Meetings chaired by others

What about meetings you attend that are chaired by others? When these are overlong and under-effective, what can you do? You're certainly more limited than you are with your own meetings, but you can still make some worthwhile time savings.

» If there's nothing in it for you, get out of the meeting if you possibly can.

» If only some of the agenda items are relevant to you, ask for these to be covered first so you can leave part way through the meeting (another strategically timed meeting or appointment may help with this).

» Help the chairperson along if they aren't doing their job properly (but be subtle; you want them to feel grateful, not resentful that you're treading on their toes). If the discussion is repeating itself, summarize it with an air of finality. If someone is talking too much, use your own skills to cut them off politely, rather than waiting on the off chance that the chairperson might do it.

KEY LEARNING POINTS
Goal-setting

» Clear goals ensure that you spend your time on the most effective tasks.

» Write down goals that are measurable, challenging and achievable.

» Give yourself a clear timeframe in which to achieve your goals.

Traveling time

» Choose the most effective form of transport for each journey.

» Find ways to be as productive as possible while traveling.

Dealing with deadlines

» Don't agree to deadlines you can't meet.

» Break major deadlines down into a series of manageable mini-deadlines.

Spending less time in meetings

» Don't hold unnecessary meetings.

» Circulate a detailed agenda, including timings, well in advance.

» Insist others are organized about requesting agenda items, submitting paperwork for circulation, and so on.

» Keep the meeting under control.

» Try to avoid going to meetings you don't need to attend.

The State of the Art

"For over half a century now I've watched office obesity develop into a full-blown, crippling disease. As our office clutter mounts, we're ever more intimidated and frustrated by it. We engineer drainage and removal of water and liquid wastes from society to prevent hazardous buildup, but the effluent that pours into our offices – paper – is never flushed out."

Don Aslett

There have been radical developments in the workplace in recent years – from styles of working to new technology – and time management has changed out of all recognition. There are now so many ways of getting more out of your time, it's a wonder that we're still working as many hours as we are. The fact is, of course, that we are expected – by ourselves as much as by others – to get through far more work than in the past. The new tools and innovative ways of working should help us to do just that.

While workplace developments have given us huge benefits in terms of productive output, they have also brought a particular danger: if we put all the new efficiencies into our work time, it can add to our stress levels; constant stress inevitably leads to health problems. It's true that if we maintain our working hours at the same level, we can hugely increase our effectiveness. But we do it by setting tighter schedules and targeting more tasks – because we *can*. As soon as anything goes wrong, the work overload builds up at a frightening and overwhelming pace.

This isn't how it was meant to be. The modern approach to time management recognizes that relaxed and happy people work far more effectively, and that work success should not be achieved at the expense of family, social life and leisure time. A rounded life – successful in all areas, not only in work – is what makes for productive managers and staff during working hours.

The answer is to take the huge time savings that are now available – through flexible styles of working and new technology – and distribute them across your life as a whole. If you use the latest tools to make you more productive at work, you can cut down on your overlong working hours, and give yourself more time at home. This will make you happier and more relaxed and, as a result, more effective at work.

Managers have a responsibility to their employees, too. The more help you can give them by way of better time management tools and practices, the more effective they will be. Help them to spread the benefits between work and home, and they will be less stressed as a result. You will find yourself managing a happier working team, and enjoying more tangible positive results, such as lower staff turnover and higher productivity.

FLEXIBLE WORKING

In the old days, all workers clocked on and off at the same time every day. Their working day ran from 9am to 5pm, or whatever. Times may have changed, but old attitudes have hung on for too long in many organizations, with no justification. If someone is more productive in the morning, wouldn't it make more sense to let them work from 8am to 4pm? We'd get more work out of them and they'd feel more satisfied with their job. If someone is perfect for the job but simply can't get to work until 10am, after the school run, wouldn't it make more sense to let them start late than to turn them down and offer the job to someone less suitable?

Countless studies have shown that happier staff are more productive and more motivated, and certainly those organizations that adopt flexible working practices would bear this out. At Asda, the UK supermarket chain owned by Wal-Mart, a whole raft of flexible practices has seen a dramatic rise in staff retention (see Chapter 7). Flexible working makes sound economic sense.

Once you break away from the old mindset and look at what works on a practical level, rather than sticking to tradition for its own sake, the old way of working actually starts to look rather daft. Surely you want people at their happiest and most productive? And you want the best people for the job – even if they can't manage the usual 9 to 5. If we invented working practices from scratch today, with modern values, we'd never dream of making everyone work exactly the same hours. Since people are all different – in their personal circumstances and their methods of working – they clearly need to work different hours to be at their best.

Obviously, there is a point beyond which flexibility ceases to be effective. If people who are supposed to work closely on the same team never actually meet, there will be problems. It will be impossible to fix meetings if the working hours of the relevant people barely overlap (remember, it's frequently near-impossible to schedule meetings *without* flexible working), and scheduling work is impractical if you don't know who is available when.

You need to set some parameters.

» The working hours of each person need to be set in advance (or any ad hoc flexibility agreed as early as possible), so that managers can schedule any tasks that need certain people to be present.
» There must be a reasonable overlap when people who work closely together are all at work at the same time. What this overlap should be will vary from case to case, but it should be agreed and stuck to.
» Team unity will suffer if any team is never all together at once. Find some time each week when everyone is together.

Essentially, any flexibility that improves time management and effectiveness is worth incorporating, and anything that damages them isn't. It's as simple as that.

Flexible working is about far more than simply starting and finishing work at different times (as you can see from the Asda case study in Chapter 7). In fact, it's as creative as you can make it, to suit your own circumstances and those of your staff. One of the most popular flexible modern practices is unpaid personal leave days. This means each employee can take time off in addition to paid holiday – and without being off sick – for anything from visiting the dentist to staying at home with an unwell child.

Most organizations that give unpaid personal leave days allocate a certain number of days to each employee to use (or not) as they wish. Some give a small number of paid personal leave days (for emergencies) and an additional number of unpaid days. This is a sensible response to modern lifestyles, with both partners often working, and no one at home to deal with plumbers, sick children, packing up to move house, or other chores.

TELEWORKING

Many organizations are more enlightened about teleworking than about flexible working hours, but it's still another modern way of working that is taking a while to catch on. There are huge advantages to be gained by working from home, both for the organization and for the worker. It's something that is often impractical for blue collar workers, but is increasingly popular for executives. If you don't already do it, you should try it, and encourage your staff to try it too.

For most people, the best way to use teleworking is part-time. Most of us need to spend some time in the office. Some meetings and discussions need to be held face-to-face, and there may be some facilities that are accessible from the office and not from home. The majority of teleworkers also find that they need the social interaction of office life; while a certain amount of teleworking is ideal for them, too much can provoke feelings of isolation and loneliness, and this can have a detrimental effect on their work as well as their mood.

Working from home for one or two days a week is ideal for most people, and carries huge benefits.

» There are fewer interruptions or distractions at home, and the productivity of teleworkers tends to rocket (by as much as 30 per cent, according to some studies).

» Morale and motivation rise. Most people enjoy working at home – at least some of the time – and also enjoy the satisfaction of being more productive. Studies show that absenteeism and stress are lower in teleworkers, and staff retention is higher.

» Teleworkers can put in more hours of work in less time. If you usually spend two hours a day commuting, working from home allows you to put in an extra hour's work each day, and gain an hour of free time too.

» Certain tasks are better suited to being done at home and these can be saved up for the days when you work out of the office. These are tasks that require little interaction with others (although you still have the phone and e-mail if you need them), but demand concentration and focus. Ideal tasks to do from home include: planning, report writing, preparing for appraisal interviews or meetings, drawing up budgets, writing proposals, online research, preparing presentations, drawing up schedules, catching up on paperwork. . .and plenty more.

Unless you are deeply incapable of self-motivation, it's hard to overstress the massive boost output you achieve when you work from home.

People who work mostly at home will tell you that, on the occasions when they go into an office, they seem to achieve as much by 11am as the regular office workers will have managed by the end of the day. If you work from home one or two days a week – and encourage your staff to do the same – you'll find it has a knock-on effect, making everyone more effective when they are in the office.

The increase in productivity (as well as in morale) makes it more than viable economically for organizations to kit out executives with all the necessary technology at home. At the least you need

» two phone lines (one for calls, one for the modem);
» an answerphone or a voicemail system;
» a computer with internet connection and printer;
» fax machine; and
» easy access to a photocopier.

The last two can be combined in one machine, perhaps with a printer too (although this means you can't receive faxes or make photocopies while printing). You might also find a scanner useful. The overall cost of the equipment is relatively low these days, and will be paid back very quickly. The savings in office costs when employees work from home are estimated at around 46 per cent.

The greatest resistance to teleworking tends to come from old-fashioned organizations and managers who fail to trust their employees. Such an attitude obviously undermines morale; no one likes to feel they're not trusted. It is also unjustified. Nowadays everyone has clear objectives and targets at work, and it's very easy to see whether they are meeting them or not. We measure people by output, not by input. If one of your team does take two-hour lunch breaks at home, but still increases their output by being at home, why should you care?

Teleworking can always be tested initially on a small scale, providing an opportunity for any problems to be detected and ironed out. If you have a team of people who would be happier and more effective if they spent some time working at home, you could allow them to work from home, say, one day a fortnight. If this works well, deal with any potential downsides, such as difficulty scheduling team meetings, and so on, and then increase teleworking for those people who enjoy it and who become more productive.

NEW TECHNOLOGY

It's not only attitudes and working practices that are revolutionizing time management; technological developments are playing their part, too.

Handheld personal computers

There has been a huge rise in recent years in the popularity of handheld computers, which carry just about all the information you need to keep you organized, and help you use your time effectively. Many of the tiny battery-operated computers are small enough to fit in a pocket.

Primarily, the handheld computer functions as a lightweight personal organizer, containing your diary, address and phone book. It may also provide you with an interactive "to do" list, memo pad or voice-memo, and features such as expense reporting. On top of this, many handhelds contain built-in modems, enabling you to send and pick up e-mails, send faxes and go online when you're away from the office.

Along with laptop computers, handheld personal computers are a hugely effective way to keep organized and in touch, and can save you masses of time. You can send and receive e-mails while you're stuck in traffic or waiting for a train, make notes and record ideas as you travel, and use your Internet connection to do research or to check on travel timetables.

Software to get you organized

Handheld personal computers are a huge boon to the busy manager. But their capabilities pale into insignificance when you look at what some of the latest software can do for streamlining your time.

The most common are organizer software packages, also known as "Personal Information Managers" or "PIMs". These perform many of the same functions as a paper-based personal planner, but they do it far more efficiently, saving you time. Different PIMs have varying features, which may include some or all of the following.

» Automatic rollover of any undone items on your "to do" list, saving you the job of writing them out again.
» Automatic entry of regular events, such as weekly or monthly meetings, in your electronic diary, avoiding the necessity of repeating entries.

» Fast finding of information from your diary, old "to do" lists or memos, using a keyword search.
» The ability to print out any information you need to take out of the office with you.
» Network PIMs make everyone's diary accessible to the group, allowing easy scheduling of meetings at a time everyone can make.
» Network PIMs also provide access to the company phonebook and other data.
» Newer PIMs include a paging function, which you can set to flash reminders up on the screen or to send a text message to your pager.
» More recent versions also allow you to click on a contact name stored in the PIM and to ask your system to dial it automatically.

PIMs are at their most effective if everyone on the team uses them and you have a networked system. This means that when you use, for example, the group diary function to schedule meetings, you know that everyone concerned uses their PIM and keeps their diary up to date.

If you are planning to invest in PIMs for your team, make sure you pick one that is easy to use and gives plenty of personal benefits and time savings to your team members. In this way, they will be motivated to "buy into" the system.

As well as investing in specific time management software such as PIMs, it's also important to have the fastest and most effective software for regular use – spreadsheet programs, word-processing software, and so on. It can sometimes seem frustrating to have to keep upgrading your equipment, but it is frequently worth it. New developments take place all the time, and improvements in software may save you huge amounts of time. For example, just a few years ago you couldn't work on a PC at the same time as using it to print out. Keep track of the available upgrades, and what they can do for you, and make the decision to invest in any that can save you time.

It's not enough simply to have the software, of course. You also have to know how to use it. Most software today seems to come with a million and one features, the majority of which you will never need. But, all too often, there are dozens of features that could be huge time-savers – if only you knew they were there, and how to use them. Investment in upgraded software is often wasted unless you also invest in training – for you and any staff who have upgraded – which will help you to get the most from it. From shortcut keys to completely new features, the right software makes a huge impact on time management, so long as you actually use it to its full potential.

GOING GLOBAL

Cultural differences

Modern technology has enabled us to globalize business in a way we could never have imagined in the past. E-mail and the Internet give us all effective 24-hour access to each other, with minimal delay. But, even though we can all communicate with each other fast, and whenever we want, we all have different perceptions of time and how it should be managed.

The fact that we now live in a "global village" can lead us to assume that, especially in business, we all have the same approach to time. This can lead to problems when working with people and organizations from other cultures. In many Western business cultures, good timekeeping is considered essential. Arriving 20 minutes late for a meeting would be considered extremely poor form in Germany, for example, where punctuality indicates trustworthiness as well as politeness. In many parts of Africa, however, it would be regarded as standard practice.

Westerners can be infuriated by the waste of their time that business people from other cultures often impose. After all, the expression "time is money" originated in the US (see Chapter 3). There, the attitude is that anyone who wastes your time is costing you money. Business people from other cultures, however, can find the Western attitude illogical, and are quite shocked when Westerners take offence at timekeeping habits that, to them, are perfectly normal.

And it's not simply a matter of whether or not you're on time for appointments. In some countries, such as Korea, for example, business arrangements are left until the last minute. This is an extension of the traditional practice of issuing invitations to social events very close to the date, so that the guest won't forget to turn up. In business, it translates into fixing meetings and appointments as late as possible. This may work fine in dealings with Latin American or Middle Eastern countries, and even many of the southern European nations, as well as

Korea, but it doesn't go down well with most people from the US or the rest of Europe.

Monochronic and polychronic time

Cultural differences can become even more of a time management headache when it comes to scheduling delivery times. Businesspeople in many cultures would never promise a delivery time that they didn't believe they could meet. In others, however, a delivery date is something that is promised so that the customer will place the order, not because it can actually be met. Doing business across cultures can lead to real scheduling problems if managers are unaware of the attitude their customer or supplier may have in respect of meeting deadlines.

According to E.T. Hall (see Chapter 8), cultures deal with time in one of two ways: they either use monochronic time or polychronic time. Monochronic time is linear, and only one thing can be done at any one time. Time is scheduled carefully, and specific amounts of time are allocated to each task. This is typical of countries such as the US, Australia, Germany, Switzerland and northern Europe.

Polychronic cultures regard time very differently. Lots of tasks can be done at the same time, and they take as long as they take. Times specified for appointments are considered approximate, not precise. One of the reasons for this is that these cultures place a higher emphasis on interpersonal relationships, with people taking priority over time.

What's the upshot of all this? We're at a turning point in terms of business perceptions of time. We've progressed to the point where we can do business with organizations all around the world, but we haven't yet established a global business culture. Attitudes to time are very different, and we need to recognize this when we do business with other countries. There is no right and wrong, but if you don't recognize and adapt to the culture of your business associates, your own time management practices could be seriously affected.

We need to research the culture of organizations we deal with overseas, if we don't already understand it. Then we should build their concept of time into our schedules, from meeting times to crucial delivery dates.

There is a general feeling that the move towards globalization is being driven chiefly by countries such as the US and Germany, with their monochronic view of time, and that these cultures will eventually set the dominant tone for doing business. But this hasn't happened yet. For the time being, it's essential to adopt a policy of acceptance towards cultures that differ from our own if we want to get the most benefit out of doing business with them.

KEY LEARNING POINTS

Flexible working
» Flexible working practices make for happier and therefore more productive employees.
» Certain parameters need to be set to make flexible working practicable.

Teleworking
» Productivity increases by up to 30 per cent.
» Morale and motivation increase.
» Absenteeism and stress are reduced.
» Savings in office costs are around 46 per cent.
» Trust shouldn't be an issue; the issue is simply whether workers still meet their targets.

New technology
» Handheld personal computers.
» Software to help you get organized.

Going global
» Different cultures have different attitudes to time.
» Globalization affects timekeeping, scheduling meetings, and meeting deadlines.
» Cultures work on either monochronic and polychronic time.

In Practice: Time Management Success Stories

» Asda
» Jim Denney
» Robert Paterson

"Time waste differs from material waste in that there can be no salvage."

Henry Ford

ASDA

In the early 1990s, UK supermarket chain Asda recognized a need to act in order to improve staff retention and reduce absenteeism. In 1995, the company made a decision to adopt more family-friendly policies. It was employing over 100,000 workers in its 240 stores, and 74 per cent of these were women.

More flexible working practices were introduced in order to encourage women to join – and stay with – the organization. It costs as much as £10,000 to replace a member of staff who doesn't return to work after maternity leave, so Asda wanted to come up with new policies that would attract such employees back to work. Supermarkets also employ plenty of students, so they wanted to encourage this sector to work for them too.

Asda introduced a wide range of flexible practices to boost staff retention and morale, and to accommodate the particular needs of their staff.

» Childcare leave: parents are able to stop work for a short period during the summer holidays, without loss of benefits.
» Shift swapping: allowing staff to be absent from work for specific domestic reasons.
» School starter scheme: allowing parents to take half a day off on their child's first day at school.
» 'Benidorm' and carer's leave: up to three months unpaid leave regardless of length of service, without loss of benefits.
» Paternity leave: regardless of length of service, five days paid leave and up to three months unpaid.
» Childcare information: a childcare partnership with a charity, linking all stores with local childcare information.
» Parental leave: between one and four weeks unpaid leave a year for coping with children's problems or illness.
» Maternity leave: statutory leave plus time off for antenatal care and further periods off after the birth.

» Adoption leave: up to three months.
» Emergency family leave: a flexible approach to time off for family emergencies, for example, if a child is taken ill at school.
» Career breaks: after five years' service, a break of up to two years for several reasons, including caring for children or further education.
» Study leave: to help students, allowing them to work fewer hours during term time and more in the holidays.
» Store swap: students can work at one store in term time, and another when they go home for the holidays.

These flexible practices, many of them highly original, have done the trick for Asda and attracted many staff both to join the company and to stay. As a result, staff turnover has dropped four per cent since 1995, and absenteeism has reduced by one per cent. The results go to show that being more flexible about managing the workforce's time pays off for everyone.

ASDA

Timeline
» 1995: Adopts flexible working practices
» 1998: *Parents at Work* Employer of the Year (large company category)
» 1999: First-ever UK supermarket store manager job share launched
» 1999: Asda acquired by Wal-Mart
» 2001: Fifth-best employer in *Sunday Times* survey

Time management insights
» Asda recognized that, with a high proportion of women in its workforce, it had to make it easy for them to work, while bringing up a family at the same time. Asda concentrated on policies that suited its own workforce, and put together a popular and workable raft of flexible working practices.
» Asda has been highly creative in finding innovative ways of working that are customized to suit its own employees. As with all the best time management measures, Asda's policy paid off in

lower staff turnover and absenteeism. Far from increasing Asda's costs, this enlightened approach has given benefits all round, to the organization and its employees.

JIM DENNEY'S BLOCK-BUSTERS

California-based Jim Denney is a successful full-time writer. He used to write part-time only, earning his main living in graphic design and advertising. He wrote and sold a number of articles to various magazines, but felt he had to be "inspired" to write, and couldn't produce sufficient output to make a living solely from his writing.

After his first few successes, however, he really wanted to change profession to become a writer full-time. He took the decision to give up the day job, and devote himself to his new career. He recalls,

> "One of the fortunate things that happened to me early on was that I was introduced in 1990 to Bert Decker and his wife, motivational speaker Dru Scott Decker. From Bert and Dru, I learned life-changing principles of time management, motivation, organization and concentration that probably saved my professional life."

In order to overcome problems with his writing, Jim uses a number of time management techniques that would be useful to anyone in a management role, too. As well as applying to business writing, such as reports and proposals, almost all these techniques also represent valuable ways of gaining more time in running projects, getting on with disagreeable tasks, and running a department.

> "I haven't been troubled by writer's block for nearly 10 years. But I remember what it feels like. Boy, do I remember! You sit at the keyboard and either nothing flows on to the screen – or what does flow on to the screen would be better suited to flow down a stormdrain. It's frustrating. It's scary. It's intimidating. It shakes your self-confidence.
> "Writer's block used to side-track me from my goals – but no more. I've been writing full-time for over a dozen years now, and

in that time I haven't been "blocked" once. I've been stumped or frustrated for an hour or two, but I no longer get "blocked" for a day or longer. The reason for that, I believe, is twofold: first, I can't afford the luxury of writer's block. If I don't produce, I don't get paid. I have to generate four or five books a year in order to pay the mortgage, feed my kids, and keep electrical current coursing through the innards of my computer. There's a lot to be said for having the wolf camped out on your welcome mat."

Jim has acquired effective "block-busting" techniques to get him through the rough spots.

1. The Grab 15 Principle

Many writers get blocked for weeks, months, even years at a time because they are waiting for the perfect time to write: "I don't have time to write a book right now, I'm just too busy." We wait until we have a few days or a few weeks of spare time, and then we think we're going to get that book written! But that golden, hoped-for spare time never arrives. The fact is, most of us fail to realize how much irreplaceable time slips right through our fingers.

Working with business guru Bert Decker and his wife, time management expert Dru Scott, I learned a priceless secret that has put hours and hours of extra writing time into my life: The Grab 15 Principle. In fact, I recently completed a 450-page novel that I wrote entirely using the Grab 15 Principle. Here's how it works.

Decide what project you are going to devote yourself to, then make a commitment that you will "Grab 15" every day without fail – that is, you will devote 15 minutes of every day to that cherished dream project, no matter what. No matter how busy your day, you promise yourself that your head won't hit the pillow that night until you have spent at least 15 minutes on it.

There are several reasons why this technique is so powerful.

» All those little 15-minute chunks of time add up – *fast!* As Dru Scott points out, even if you take Sundays off from your "Grab 15" commitment, those 15 minutes a day times 6 days equals 90 minutes a week – or a whopping 78 hours in a year!

» It boosts your creativity. Ideas and insights come to you in the shower, on your commute, and over breakfast, because your project is continually on your mind.

» You find it hard to stop at 15 minutes!

2. Withdraw briefly

Sometimes you get blocked when you press too hard. You get too close to the problem and can't see your way through the tangle of ideas, thoughts, and feelings. You become stressed. You need a break. You need to withdraw for just a bit. My favorite withdrawal techniques include

» walking away from the computer, going into the living room and lying down on the couch, putting my feet up, closing my eyes, and just clearing my mind; day-dreaming, letting my thoughts float, meditating, or praying;

» putting on my jogging suit and running;

» taking a hot shower; or

» listening to music.

When you withdraw, avoid all input that would distract. You want to back off from your project – but not too far. Turning on the TV or talk radio will take your mind completely off your writing project.

3. Leave a gap and move on

Often, when I come to a tough passage in a book, I say to myself, "This is tough now, but it will be easier later." So I insert a note at that point that says "[TO COME: SECTION ON BLAH-BLAH-BLAH.]" I usually write it all in caps so it stands out, and I sometimes use the bookmark feature in my word processor to make it easy to find. Later, when I come back to that difficult passage, I have the advantage of having written most of the book to the very end. That gives me an overview of the entire book that I didn't have at the time when I left the gap. Sometimes I even find out that the passage I was trying to write would have been redundant or unnecessary.

4. Write garbage and move on

Writing garbage and moving on is a lot like leaving a gap and moving on. You write it, you hate it, but you don't worry about it. You say to yourself, "It's lousy, but what the hey! I'll fix it later."

I know a lot of people who are obsessive-compulsive about their writing. They must have every sentence buffed and polished to perfection before they can move on to the next sentence. They can't leave gaps. They can't write garbage and move on. They demand first-draft perfection. Such people write themselves into an early grave, and their output tends to be very constipated.

5. Build your book, story, or article on an outline

A lot of people don't like to outline their projects. "That's too confining, too limiting," they say. I think that attitude shows a lack of discipline, a lack of seriousness and realism about the writing process. I've learned that you've got to know where you're going or you'll never get there.

When I first got the idea for the novel I recently finished, the basic storyline came to me in a rush. I got horizontal on my living room couch and figured out the major high points, scenes and plot twists in the space of about an hour – just lying there with my eyes closed. Then I sat down at the computer and hammered out an outline, about three pages worth.

Over the next few months, I grew that outline. But I never felt limited or bound by it. I could explore new ideas, take plot detours, add or delete characters or subplots – but everything I wrote took place within a structure that gave me a sense of direction, a goal to aim for.

I follow pretty much the same route with my nonfiction books. I assemble an outline, grow that into a book proposal, sell the proposal to the publisher, and then I grow the proposal into a book. Far from being limiting or rigid, it's a very organic and satisfying way to write (notice that organized and organic come from the same root word).

6. Stop while you're on a roll

This sounds crazy, but it really works. I keep a disciplined writing time, and I try to make sure I'm in the middle of an easy section when I quit for the day. That way, I know that when I sit down at the computer the next day, I won't feel daunted by the challenge. Instead, I'll feel eager to jump right in and keep going.

Use momentum to your advantage. If possible, try to get through difficult sections while you've got energy and momentum working for you. Save the easy stuff for getting started the next time you start writing.

7. Always write forward, never backward

I know writers and wannabe writers who continually obsess over the first few paragraphs they've written and never get around to writing the rest of the book. I think a lot of writers get blocked because they think too much about what they've written and not enough about what they have yet to write. Trust me. You want to write great stuff? Then keep writing forward, and don't look back.

8. When you start your writing time, try backing up a few paragraphs

Remember that I said you should always write forward, never back? Well, this is a slight exception to that rule. Sometimes, if it's hard to get into the flow of the book from a standing start, it helps to back up just a couple paragraphs and take a running start. Just re-read and polish up a few paragraphs, get your creative juices flowing, re-capture the momentum and the mood you had during your last writing session – then keep moving forward.

9. Use "heart-starters" to crank up your enthusiasm

A "heart-starter" is a motivational phrase, a motivational book, an upbeat song on a CD – anything that lubricates your emotions and imagination so that the words can flow. I keep a terrific heart-starter on top of my computer case – a book called *Dare To Be a Great Writer* by Leonard Bishop (Writer's Digest Books, 1988). It's comprised of 329 short essays on a variety of writing topics, all of them practical and essential, but none of which take more than a minute to read. I often open the book, select an essay at random, read it, and then close the book feeling revved up and ready to write.

10. Believe you can do it

Act on the belief that you are a good writer creating great work – even if you don't believe it. Make a decision to sit down and write, whether you feel like it or not, whether you are "inspired" or not. Act first, and the feelings will follow. Some people wait for the *feelings* of a writer to come before they exhibit the *behavior* of a writer. Very self-defeating.

This is crucial to understand: *feelings follow behavior*. So act like a writer. Place your fingers on your keyboard – and produce! Only when you *act* like a writer and *produce* like a writer will you truly *feel* like a writer.

Those are my 10 block-busters. Nothing magical – just practical. I'm a writer today because these block-busters work. I know they'll work for you.

© Jim Denney

This material is reproduced by kind permission of Jim Denney

TIME MANAGEMENT INSIGHTS: JIM DENNEY

» Jim Denney grasped the basic principle that you can't just go with the flow; you have to take active steps to manage your time. By imposing on himself new ways of working, he learnt to conquer the writer's block that had troubled him in the past.

» Jim armed himself with a wide range of techniques, which, put together, are far more powerful than any one on its own. This means that whatever problem he encounters, he has a tool for resolving it.

» Several of Jim Denney's methods involve dealing with that point at which you can see your way forward. Whether you withdraw, skip a section or produce garbage briefly (with a view to going back and filling in later), these techniques are equally valuable when you encounter a sticky stage in a project or other kind of task.

ROBERT PATERSON

Just a few years ago, international investment banker Robert Paterson was told by his doctor that he was grossly obese. He knew he had to do something, so he used time management techniques to reduce his weight. Not only that, but the changes he made led to a major lifestyle overhaul, and he ended up running his own business. Here's his story.

I was coming back from Havana, an international investment banker, looking for another job in the City. I weighed over 22 stone. My chances of getting another job, the way I looked, were slender. Worse, even if I got another job, the doctors had been telling me for years that, unless I lost some weight, I would not see out a normal career, let alone old age.

But where was I to start?

I had, over the years, tried many different diets. They all worked. They all succeeded in getting weight off. But none of them succeeded in enabling me to keep it off. So, rather than go for another crash diet, I decided to analyze why anyone, including myself, becomes overweight. I came up with only four reasons.

1 Genetics – nothing you can do about that, at present. It's like getting a bad hand at cards, but you still have to play the hand. Being genetically predisposed to obesity does not preclude you from a healthy life. There are excellent scientific studies on this.
2 Nutrition – too much, relative to exercise.
3 Exercise – not enough, in relation to nutrition.
4 Mindset – the key factor that is so readily overlooked. Many will say if you want to lose weight and get fitter it's just a question of willpower. I can assure you most overweight, unfit individuals have buckets of willpower. That is not what enables you to succeed, long term.

Armed with this information I decided to develop my understanding of the three areas that I could manage: nutrition, exercise and mindset.

Where was I to go for help?

First, I tried some friendly and well-known "slimmers' clubs." All were most welcoming – especially as I was the token male. And that is just the point. I wanted to belong to a group, but, as a man, I felt I did not belong there. And most of the people I met at these meetings had a totally different lifestyle from mine. They could get down to the church hall every Wednesday night. They had a set pattern to their day. They had time often to shop and cook. My life revolved around my work – tight schedules, business travel and entertaining.

I joined a gym, but I soon concluded that there was little time available for exercise in an average business day.

I reflected on what had and what had not worked for me. All the diet programs I could find really concentrated on one, or at most two, key areas of weight management. They either focused on nutrition (slimmers' clubs) or exercise (gyms and health clubs). Hardly any touched on mindset.

What was worse is that each program gave you *its* formula for managing *your* weight. Frankly, you can only follow another person's program for so long – being human, we tend to go back to our old tried and tested ways – and that is where most diets fail. You just cannot stick to them, because they don't address all the issues that need to be tackled, and they are not tailored to your own lifestyle. One person may want to run a marathon and another may want to walk the dog three times a week. They may both want to get healthier and fitter, but their ultimate goals are totally different. Clearly, their nutrition and exercise need to be different, too.

In some desperation I decided that the only way forward was to "invent" my own diet. And that is when I started to look at what skills I had for doing this. I knew how to run a company; could my body be managed along similar lines?

I started putting this to the test.

First, I took on a group of consultants to help me run the business. They included a nutritionist (a State Registered Dietician), a personal trainer and a life coach (for the mindset). I told them what my goals and objectives were and I wrote my own "business plan" around my body, including a "history of the company". What had I done in managing this business before and what could I learn from those experiences? Was I a fair-weather sportsman? Was that one of my weaknesses? One of my strengths was that I could manage time well. I had been a time manager, in my business life, for years.

Now I was starting to see how my business skills could be used in the management of my body. I went further – I realized that culture change would be necessary. It would be painful but I had managed culture change before. I knew that, as in business, my actions in managing my body would affect others. I needed to manage those people's expectations. How was I going to persuade my old drinking buddies that I was about to change? What benefits would my partner get out of the process (other than being forced to give up eating in good restaurants?)?

Then there was the management of the business. What did I really want to produce? Driving down my stock levels (reducing weight) would turn me into a more efficient company with a healthier bank balance, but what was I going to produce? I decided I would be an athlete, albeit an amateur one. I set my mind to running my first marathon, then my second, then triathlon. Now it's bikehiking, a charitable event I set up with the Family Heart Association, as a way of giving something back: www.greatbikehire.co.uk.

Time management was the most important skill that I brought to bear in running my body business. I knew there were certain vital areas that I had to cover in managing my body, all of which would be time-related.

1 Planning and doing exercise – regularly. This was achieved by looking at exercise as I would look at a business meeting. I made it sacrosanct. I would get up 45 minutes earlier each day (much easier when I cut down on alcohol) and went to bed just a little earlier. I would get straight out of bed, into my kit, do my exercise routine, then jump under the shower – a huge time saving all round. The planning ensured that I got most of my regular training done every day. Most people tend to train after work – this has the benefit of being a great stress reliever, but it is more time-consuming than the morning routine and does not always guarantee success when a busy schedule gets in the way.

2 Planning and cooking meals. I decided that I would plan my meals a week ahead, then I would cook double the quantity of any given recipe and freeze the result in meal-sized portions. I would only need to cook once or, at most, twice a week. I also "invented" some really quick but healthy meals, governed by some basic rules. They could never take more than 30 minutes, because that was how long the alternative (a take-away pizza or an Indian meal) would take to deliver. They also had to be well balanced and healthy and all the ingredients had to be available at any late-night supermarket, in case I needed to pick them up on the way home from work.

3 Monitoring and measuring results. You wouldn't expect to change a corner shop into a multinational enterprise overnight. Nor would you expect your abused body to perform like an Olympian in just a few weeks. Time management enabled me to take things at a gradual and steady pace. It took me six months training to run my first 10K race and a further 12 months to run my first marathon. I knew that

my weight loss would be gradual. Companies do not review their health and profitability on a daily basis, yet most weight managers jump on the bathroom scales and expect to get an instant result. When, in spite of doing everything right, the scales show a slight increase, many give up and go back to their old habits. Would you do that in your business?

Among the other management skills that I brought to my weight management business were management of change and management of my internal self.

Change is a four-step process.

1 Dissatisfaction with the present position.
2 A clear and attractive vision of the future.
3 Stepping stones between where you are today and your vision of where you want to be in the future.
4 An unshakeable belief that the process is possible and that crossing the stepping stones will get you there.

If any of the steps are missed, the result will be ultimate failure.

I also needed to manage my internal self. My internal dialogue was worse than judge and jury put together. We all have rules for how we handle situations and I started to look at what sort of "culture" my body business had. If I had a young manager who was still learning his skills, would I pounce on him every time he made a mistake? What would that do to my business? In respect of my body, I would find myself being that "bullying manager" every time I "slipped up". By taking the approach of the caring and educating line manager I suddenly discovered that, when I came off track with my program, I learnt from the process rather than beating myself up for getting it wrong.

Recognizing the isolation men experience when confronting weight management issues, and understanding how similar the process can be to running a company, I decided in 1999 to found "Warriors", the only weight management program in Britain for men. Initially London-based, it has now expanded to Manchester and Glasgow.

The 10-week program starts with a one-day workshop, followed by a 10-day period spent developing the body "business plan". Thereafter, clients receive on-going support via e-mail on a weekly basis. Further assistance is also provided through personal trainers, life coaches and nutritionists. For full details, go to www.warriors.org.uk. My book *Warriors* (Piatkus) is available from all major UK book outlets.

TIME MANAGEMENT INSIGHTS: ROBERT PATERSON

» Robert Paterson discovered how wide-reaching time management principles can be. Many people were already using them to organize their diary or schedule their time, but Robert recognized that he could use them to lose weight and become healthier.

» Some people struggle with time management because they feel that they are being subjected to methods that simply don't suit them. The whole issue of dieting had been much the same for Robert, until he found his own approach, which suited *him*. The discipline of time management incorporates a huge number of techniques for helping you get more done in less time; part of the trick is to recognize which of the tools and methods will work for *you*.

» Robert applied his time management techniques across the board, to his daily schedule, to monitoring his progress and even to cooking his evening meals. Once you start applying time management principles to your life, they can usefully extend into every aspect of it.

Key Concepts and Thinkers in Time Management

"He who knows how not to waste time can do just about anything; and he who knows how to make use of time will be lord of whatever he wants."

Leon Alberti

A GLOSSARY FOR TIME MANAGEMENT

80/20 rule – Also known as the Pareto Principle. In terms of time management, it states that 80 per cent of the productive work is achieved in 20 per cent of the time.

Action list – A daily list of tasks to be achieved by the end of the day, organized according to priority. Also known as a *"to do" list* or *daily task list*.

Activity log – A log of activities throughout the day, marking how long each activity takes, in order to track how time is spent. Also known as a work log, or as time tracking.

Daily planner – Similar to a diary, a planner has plenty of space for each day, and provides not only space to write appointments and reminders, but also space to write down goals and objectives.

Daily task list – A daily list of tasks to be achieved by the end of the day, organized according to priority. Also known as a *"to do" list* or *action list*.

Delegation – The skilled exercise of passing on both a task and the responsibility for that task to a subordinate, while still retaining overall responsibility and monitoring the subordinate's progress.

Effectiveness – Effectiveness is different from efficiency. Efficiency means getting through the work in good time; effectiveness means getting through the *right* work in good time. It focuses not only on how the work is done, but also on what work it is. Effective work is work that helps to achieve *goals* and *objectives*.

Goal – A clear target to work towards, which should be specific, measurable, challenging but achievable, and should have a deadline by which you intend to achieve it. *Goals* and *objectives* are similar, but the term *goal* is generally applied to more long-term targets.

Important tasks – In terms of time management, important tasks are specifically those that help to further *goals* and *objectives*.

Marginal time – Time that has been allocated to specific tasks but becomes available, albeit with constraints. For example, time spent waiting for someone who is late for an appointment, or time spent in traffic jams. This time can be used effectively for other tasks.

Objective – A clear target to work towards, which should be specific, measurable, challenging but achievable, and should have a deadline by which you intend to achieve it. *Goals* and *objectives* are similar, but the term *objective* is generally applied to shorter-term targets.

Parkinson's Law – "Work expands to fill the time available." In terms of time management, this means that time should be allocated carefully; any tasks that are allocated more time than they need will take more time than they need.

PIMs – Personal Information Managers: software that helps you to manage your time (see Chapter 6).

Prioritizing – Ordering tasks in the most effective way, so that the most important and most urgent tasks are dealt with first.

Time tracking – Keeping a log of activities throughout the day, marking how much time is spent on each, in order to track how you spend your time. Also known as a work log, or activity log.

"To do" list – A daily list of tasks to be achieved by the end of the day, organized according to priority. Also known as an *action list* or *daily task list*.

Work log – A log of activities throughout the day, marking how much time is spent on each, in order to track how you spend your time. Also known as an activity log, or as time tracking.

KEY CONCEPTS

Goal-setting

See Chapter 6. Setting goals is essential to the modern approach to time management. Unless you know where you're headed, how can you tell that you are expending your efforts in the right direction? Goal-setting ensures that all those techniques for using time efficiently are also *effective* – in other words, they help you to achieve your core objectives.

Prioritizing

In order to work effectively, you have to make sure that the most important tasks are the ones you work on first. But defining tasks by importance alone doesn't take into account the issue of urgency. Even unimportant tasks have to be dealt with first, if they are urgent.

In his book, *The 7 Habits of Highly Effective People*, Stephen R. Covey recommends a matrix of prioritization (Table 8.1).

Table 8.1   Covey's matrix of prioritization.

	Urgent	Not urgent
Important	I	II
Not important	III	IV

In Quadrant I of the matrix of prioritization, we should put all those activities that are both important *and* urgent, for example, completing a report that is due today. In Quadrant II we put everything that is important but *not* urgent, such as planning or learning new skills that will help us achieve our goals. Quadrant III should contain urgent but *not* important activities; these include interruptions, some meetings, and activities that do not further our goals but are urgent. In Quadrant IV we put all the activities that are neither important nor urgent, for example, some phone calls and mail, time-wasters, and so on.

The number of activities in Quadrant I (important *and* urgent) can be hugely reduced by effective planning and by tackling most of these tasks while they are still in Quadrant II (important and *not* urgent). The majority of time should be spent working on Quadrant II activities.

Planning

The concept of planning is central to time management. We need to allocate time specifically for the purpose of planning – in other words, to allow time for allocating the rest of our time. Only by thinking through activities in terms of priority, and the time they will take, can we draw up effective diaries and schedules, to ensure that our time is spent as productively as possible.

Delegation

(See Chapter 10.) At managerial level, where time management really becomes an essential skill, it goes hand in hand with the skill of delegation. If you have too much work you cannot hope to get through it all in the time available, no matter how effectively you use your time. The answer is to reduce the workload, and delegation is the most effective way to do this. Not only does good delegation cut down on the number of tasks you have to get through, it also helps to develop junior staff and extend their skills.

KEY THINKERS

Don Aslett

Don Aslett is a world authority on cleaning, and this specialization has led to his becoming an expert on organizing and decluttering the office.

Aslett was born in Idaho, where he grew up on a farm. In order to pay his way through college, he set up a cleaning company, which was so successful that it became his full-time business after his graduation.

Aslett has become a well-known figure in the US, having written over 30 books, including *Clutter's Last Stand* and *The Office Clutter Cure*, and made numerous media appearances. His personal style and humor make him a popular campaigner for decluttering our lives. Having started out in the cleaning business, he has an unusual angle on time management. As a successful businessman, he also knows his stuff when it comes to organizing and bringing his principles of space-clearing to the office.

Aslett doesn't necessarily offer any extraordinary new insights into the organizational aspects of time management, but his humor and down-to-earth approach make his books and broadcasts extremely approachable.

Arnold Bennett

One of the earliest proponents of time management skills, Arnold Bennett's book *How to Live on Twenty-Four Hours a Day* was published in 1907. Popular with many businessmen of the time, the book ran to 14 editions in the US. Henry Ford is known to have issued 500 of his managers with a copy each.

Picking up on the principles of his earlier compatriot, Benjamin Franklin, Bennett also argued that time is money. He wrote: "Why not concern yourself more with 'How to live on a given income of time' instead of 'How to live on a given income of money'? Money is far commoner than time. When one reflects, one perceives that money is just about the commonest thing there is. The supply of time, though gloriously regular, is cruelly restricted. We shall never have any more time. We have, and we have always had, all the time there is."

Stephen R. Covey

One of the most successful time management thinkers of current times, Stephen R. Covey wrote the worldwide best-seller *The 7 Habits of Highly Effective People*, which has sold over 12 million copies. Together with Hyrum W. Smith, Covey runs Franklin Covey, one of the world's biggest time management organizations (see Chapter 9). For more information on Stephen R. Covey, see Chapter 3.

Edward T. Hall

Born in 1914, E.T. Hall is an expert in cultural differences. The three concepts he singles out for study of such differences are time, space and context. As far as time is concerned, he says, "Time is one of the fundamental bases on which all cultures rest and around which all activities revolve. Understanding the difference between monochronic time and polychronic time is essential to success." Monochronic time, according to Hall, is linear and divisible; events are scheduled one after another and this schedule is the top priority. Polychronic time, on the other hand, involves "the simultaneous occurrence of many things and a great involvement with people". (See Chapter 6.)

Alan Lakein

Alan Lakein developed the ABC technique for prioritizing work in order of importance. Tasks labeled "A" are the most important, followed by those marked "B" and then "C." Tasks can be subdivided by number, so that "A1" takes priority over "A2", and so on.

Although this was an important step forward in the early 1970s, it failed to distinguish between important and urgent tasks. It was Stephen R. Covey who developed the system of prioritizing according to these factors as well, which is now in common use.

Lakein made many other contributions to the discipline of time management; indeed, he has been credited with coining that very expression. His book *How to Get Control of Your Time and Your Life* has sold three million copies. In it, he argues that there is no point in saving time unless you use the time you've saved to become more successful, however you personally define "success". Taking control of your time means taking control of your life instead of being controlled.

Resources for Time Management

- » Books
- » Equipment
- » Organizations
- » Software

"I believe the 24-hour day has come to stay."

Max Beerbohm

BOOKS

Adair, John (1982) *Effective Time Management*, Pan, London

It's no surprise that this book, by management expert John Adair, has been in print for about 20 years. It is written in a straightforward, clear and common-sense style, and sets out the principles of time management in a simple way that makes them easy to understand and easy to apply.

Covey, Stephen R. (1989) *The 7 Habits of Highly Effective People*, Simon & Schuster

This world-famous book was first published in 1989, and has become a seminal work. It goes well beyond time management, taking a principle-centered approach to solving personal and professional problems. Habit 3 ("Put first things first") is the one that focuses on time management, with Covey setting out his ideas (among other things) for prioritizing work according to importance and urgency.

Mayer, Jeffrey J. (1999) *Time Management for Dummies*, IDG Books Worldwide

One of the most comprehensive guides to time management, covering everything from making your conversations more effective to choosing the right software for your computer. The author runs a Chicago-based time management consultancy, and has written widely on the subject.

Roesch, Roberta (1998) *Time Management for Busy People*, McGraw-Hill

Well set out, with plenty of up-to-date time management ideas on getting organized and on handling disruptions to a well-planned schedule, and full of checklists and "test yourself" sections.

Wright, Robert J. (1997) *Beyond Time Management, Business with Purpose*, Butterworth-Heinemann

A time management book with a twist, full of ideas for becoming more effective, but also focusing on how to live with purpose and be more fulfilled in the process. Many case studies and real-life examples to help illustrate the points and inspire the reader.

EQUIPMENT

Handheld electronic organizers are a huge boon if you spend any amount of time away from the office. The various products available are becoming smaller and more portable, and are constantly increasing their capabilities. As well as getting information on palmtop products from most of the sources listed below under "software," you'll also find the following suppliers useful.

Franklin Covey

Huge time management organization that produces many of its own products, including a range of handheld organizers and software. Unlike the suppliers of most such products, the core business of Franklin Covey is not computer technology but time management. www.franklincovey.com

Sharp USA

Leading computer manufacturer, and also one of the top manufacturers of personal organizers and handheld equipment. www.sharp-usa.com

Palm, Inc

A top producer of palmtop products, Palm Inc has an extensive range of handheld products, including portable keyboards. www.palm.com

ORGANIZATIONS

Day-Timers

Day-Timers offers numerous products aimed at helping you organize yourself and manage your time. Its products range from paper-based items – including personal organizers – to software and Internet-based materials. The organization also provides training for companies and individuals. It is based in the US, where its products are available through stores and wholesalers, and also has UK, Canadian and Australian/New Zealand divisions.

Day-Timers Website (www.daytimer.com) offers its products for sale, and also carries useful articles and other information about time management.

Franklin Covey

Franklin Covey, led by Hyrum W. Smith and Stephen R. Covey (see Chapters 3 and 8), is one of the biggest providers of time management products and training. It offers a wide range of planners, handheld organizers, software, books and training materials, as well as training and consultancy. Its Website (www.franklincovey.com) includes an online store, and also publishes discussions, articles, case studies and plenty more.

Pace Productivity

Pace Productivity offers training and consultancy services in time management. Its electronic TimeCorder device (not on general sale, but available in conjunction with the company's other services), provides a quick and simple means of producing a work log. The user simply presses a button each time there's a change in activity, rather than laboriously writing the activities all out.

Pace Productivity also has an excellent Website (www.getmoredone.com), which is full of tips and information on time management, and includes several reports, many based on Pace's own research. Topics include a discussion of the activities that workers consider to be the worst waste of time.

TMI

This international organization – TMI stands for Time Manager International – has been around since the mid-70s, teaching people to manage their time more effectively. It is at heart a training and consultancy firm, which offers a range of products alongside its services, including planners and other organizational tools. It trains over a quarter of a million people a year around the world, and its programs and products are available in over 20 languages.

The TMI Website, www.tmiworld.com, provides access to their national Websites.

managementfirst.co.uk

This Website offers information, discussions and articles about management topics, including time management. It has an extensive range of in-depth articles and links, and is well worth a visit.

mindtools.com

This Website is full of information about time management, with information, articles and time management tools, as well as an online bookstore.

SOFTWARE

Contact manager software helps you organize your address book, computerizing the information you would otherwise keep in your personal organizer. As well as holding a database of contact details, it also enables you to send e-mails and faxes, schedule meetings, track contacts and carry out other similar functions. Most contact manager software is compatible with most handheld computers, although you should always double-check this.

Personal Information Managers or PIMs (see Chapter 6) are where it's really at when it comes to using software to improve your time management. They share many features with contact managers, but they also perform other functions too. They can store a database for information as well as contacts, for example, incorporating "to do" lists, and can be set up to schedule meetings between a group of users such as an office team.

If you want a PIM that integrates with your handheld computer, or whatever hardware you use when you're away from the office, you'll need to make sure you have integrated software, so that data you enter on one automatically shows up on the other. The synchronization software that comes with most handhelds usually has fairly limited features.

If you feel a PIM is what you need to revolutionize the way you manage your time, make the effort to research the available products and choose one that really suits you. They vary considerably in style as well as in terms of features – some emulate Filofaxes, others index cards, and so on. If you make a mistake and end up having to change to a different PIM, you may experience difficulty importing the data from the old PIM to the new one.

A final note of caution regarding PIMs. Many of the newer versions on the market have no integral back-up system. This could be very risky, since your PIM is likely to contain just about everything you need to survive. Check out any PIM you're planning to buy, and make sure that you use an external back-up if necessary, in case something goes wrong.

Contact manager software programs and PIMs come on to the market with such frequency that it is important to try to keep up with developments. Use the following Websites and publications to find all the information you need to choose the best software for you.

» www.applelinks.com – Details and reviews of suitable products for you if you use a desktop or portable Apple Mac.
» www.computerworld.com – Basic information and advice, as well as reviews of the latest software on the market.
» www.consumersearch.com – Current research and side-by-side reviews for the top products, as well as comparison charts and advice on where to go for more information.
» www.emailaddresses.com – A clear, straightforward and useful round-up of the latest free calendars, "to do" lists and PIMs.
» www.palmblvd.com – Free contact managers and information on PIMs.
» www.zdnet.co.uk – Lots of information about the latest software, and wide-ranging reviews that sometimes cover PIMs.
» *CNet* magazine – All about computers and technology, with plenty of advice and information. The Website (www.cnet.com) includes software reviews and free newsletters.
» *PC World* magazine – General information, including the latest on software to improve time management. Numerous articles, reviews and free newsletters on the accompanying Website (www.pcworld.com).
» *Smart Computing* – Subscription publication that carries helpful advice, reviews and information. The extensive Website (www.smartcomputing.com) includes a full archive of every issue.

Ten Steps to Making
Time Management Work

1 Clear your desk
2 Set goals
3 Plan your diary
  » Yearly planning
  » Monthly planning
  » Weekly planning
4 Keep a daily "to do" list
5 Prioritize
  » Importance
  » Urgency
  » Order of priority
6 Delegate
7 Learn to say "no"
8 Avoid interruptions
9 Monitor your progress
10 Keep work and home separate

"Don't be afraid to give your best to what seemingly are small jobs. Every time you conquer one it makes you that much stronger. If you do the little jobs well, the big ones will tend to take care of themselves."

Dale Carnegie

Time management is a broad-reaching discipline that encompasses everything, from the big issues of core objectives and goals, down to small details, such as how to save time on the phone or when to reorder business cards. Many people, especially those with a natural tendency towards efficiency and organization, develop their own personal techniques for making better use of their time, customized to suit the activities on which they spend most time.

There are, however, certain basic principles you need to abide by if you want to practice good time management, whatever your particular role and responsibilities. Without these, you cannot hope to make the best use of your time. This chapter describes the 10 key steps you need to follow in order to be confident of squeezing more value out of the same number of hours you work now.

1. CLEAR YOUR DESK

Many people who have cluttered, untidy desks claim they work better that way. It's a great excuse after all: "I could easily tidy it, but I wouldn't work so effectively." Well, that's rubbish, I'm afraid. Actually, the vast majority of people who work in a mess have never tried working in a tidy office for more than the first few hours of any job, so how would they know which is most effective?

The truth is that having a clear, tidy office and desk leads to far more time-effective work than having a cluttered one. You can find everything you need quickly, it's all easy to use, you waste no time searching for missing paperwork or notes, and there is a strong psychological gain too: a clear desk looks straightforward and approachable, and is easy to work at. A pile of clutter is off-putting and makes it very hard to respond by clearing your mind for the start of a project or period of concentration.

Clearing your desk is not just a matter of making all those untidy piles of paperwork neater. It entails getting rid of everything unnecessary from your desk.

» Enter all notes and reminders into your diary or planner and then bin the original scraps of paper.
» Dispose of all the papers, reports, files and reading material that you've finished with and which are no longer relevant.
» Dispose of all the papers, reports, files and reading materials that you know you're never really going to get round to doing anything about.
» Get rid of all the filing and other material that needs to be kept or passed on, but not stored on your working space.

Once you've cleared everything from your desk that shouldn't be there, the next step is to make sure that everything you need frequently is there, and in the most sensible place.

» Make sure the phone is on the most convenient side of the desk for you to use it, and make sure essential items (diary and address book, hole puncher, stapler, pens, calculator, and so on) are close to hand, each in their own allocated space.
» Have a space to move your keyboard into when you're not using it so that it doesn't occupy important space when it's idle.
» Ensure that there is a large, empty working space in the middle of your desk, which is only ever occupied with the papers you're working on now. Not this week, but right now. As soon as you move on to the next item, put these papers away and clear the space again. This space should therefore be empty for much of the day – when you're working on the computer (apart from the keyboard occupying center stage), when you're out of the office, when you're between tasks.

You will save a huge amount of time by working in an organized and tidy office instead of a cluttered one. And if you find it hard to keep it tidy, make sure you clear it little and often. Make a rule that you won't leave at the end of each day until the place is tidy; do it while you're hanging on the phone, or talking informally to a colleague. If you do it regularly, it will only take five minutes a day (if that). And you'll easily save yourself even those five minutes by putting everything away where it belongs as soon as you've finished using it, so that the desk never becomes cluttered in the first place.

2. SET GOALS

Once you have a clear desk, you can start to think clearly. So sit down and work out your goals (see Chapter 5). Only by thinking through your core objectives can you be certain that you are spending your time not only efficiently, but also on the most effective, important and productive issues.

Work out what your goals are, both long term and short term. Perhaps in the long term you want to speed up delivery times in order to improve customer satisfaction. Give yourself a specific target (as we saw in Chapter 5) and a realistic timeframe in which to achieve it. In the short term, you might aim this month to find out what the constraints on delivery times are, and to talk to everyone in the department to get their views of the problem, and their suggestions for resolving it. Next month's goal might be to research how other organizations meet faster delivery targets, and to find out all the options. And so on – major long-term targets and intermediate short-term goals.

The next step is to write down your goals in your diary or planner.

3. PLAN YOUR DIARY

You might keep a diary or a planner (which includes space for writing down goals, "to do" lists, and so on). You may have this on computer (see Chapter 6) or you may use a pen and paper version. It really doesn't matter, so long as you have a system which

» works for you;
» gives you plenty of space for including reminders, to do lists, goals and so on; and
» doesn't entail having to duplicate information in more than one location, which wastes time and can cause hiccups if both locations aren't fully up to date.

What matters is that you have all your information in a single location, which has plenty of space to hold all the data you need it to.

Yearly planning

Your diary planning should begin at the start of each year (though you'll want to do it a few weeks in advance for a smooth transition into the new year). If you're doing this for the first time, go out and buy the best planner/diary/software you can find that will work for you, and start now, whatever time of year it is.

At the beginning of each year (or right now if that's where you're starting), enter in your diary or planner all the dates you already know about for the whole year:

» regular meetings;
» one-off events (trade shows or conferences, for example);
» regular events (such as a weekly lunch with your boss, or a free morning every other Monday to catch up on any backlog of work);
» holidays;
» 15 minutes of diary planning time at the start of each month;
» personal time (days off for your wedding anniversary or children's school sports day); and
» at least a whole day each month specifically for working towards your goals and developing ideas and projects for meeting your overall objectives.

Try to increase the days set aside for goal-setting and developing ideas to two or more a month, if you can. Whole days are the most productive – don't allow this time to be sliced up into several one- or two-hour sessions. Remember, this is time for doing the most important things you can possibly spend your time on at work, so treat it with respect.

Monthly planning

You scheduled yourself 15 minutes at the start of each month for diary planning, so here's what to do with it. Enter in the diary all the key tasks you didn't know about at the start of the year; you may need to make a couple of phone calls or send one or two e-mails to firm up some of these and slot them into your diary:

» selection or appraisal interviews;
» visits to customers, suppliers or advisors;
» presentations (including time to prepare);
» reports and proposals (preparation time as well as time to write the final version);
» time for delegating key tasks; and
» days you plan to work from home.

If your diary looks overfull at this point, now is the time to clear some space:

» cancel any unnecessary meetings;
» make apologies for any meetings you won't have time to attend;
» defer any tasks you need to that can reasonably be deferred;
» delegate tasks if possible (and schedule time to do this if it's going to take time); and
» streamline activities – make two trips on the same day to cut down on traveling time, for example.
» Don't, however, reduce the time you have allocated for working on core objectives and goals.

Weekly planning

You can do weekly planning every Monday morning; it should take only five minutes. Set aside time, or blocks of time, for the following:

» delegating and monitoring delegated tasks;
» catching up with phone calls (maybe 10 minutes twice a day, or however long you need);
» keeping on top of correspondence and e-mails (again, a couple of blocks of time each day);
» being available on the phone (so callers can be put off, but told they can reach you after 4.30pm, or the next morning). You need at least one period a day when people can call you, unless you're out of the office;
» being available face-to-face. Colleagues and other visitors to your office will only be deterred from interrupting you if they know that there is a time – before too long – when they will be able to speak to you. You might adopt a policy of being available every morning before 9.30am, or every afternoon after 5pm;
» dealing with miscellaneous tasks. You may not know what they're going to be, but you know they always crop up, so you'd better schedule 20 minutes a day, or the second half of Friday afternoon, or whatever works for you; and
» having a daily walkabout to keep in touch with your team.

4. KEEP A DAILY "TO DO" LIST

Each day, there are numerous tasks too small to schedule in your diary individually. Many of these are scheduled under categories – phone calls, e-mails, and so on – while others come under "miscellaneous". But how do you know what all these tasks are?

They should all be written on your "to do" list (or action list, or daily task list, whatever you prefer to call it). Every morning, when you open your diary or planner, it should contain a list of things you have to do that day: calls you have to make, facts you need to check, an order to put in for materials for next week's training session, a quote to chase up from a supplier, and all the rest of it.

So how does this list arrive in your diary? Well, you put it there.

» Every time you say to anyone, "I'll call you on Tuesday", make a note in your diary for Tuesday.
» Every time you say to anyone, "I'll make sure I get the order in on time", write yourself a note on the relevant day.
» If you say to someone, "I'll expect to hear from you by Friday", mark in Friday's diary that you need to chase it up if you haven't heard.
» As soon as you say, "I'll have it on your desk on June 30", write a note for June 30, *and* one for a day or two earlier, if you think you'll need to be forewarned.

This way, your diary will contain a list of all the things you're supposed to do, as well as those tasks that others are supposed to do for you, by the end of the day. And alongside these notes should be any relevant

» phone numbers;
» directions;
» contact names;
» prices; or
» . . . anything else you might need.

Some days, however well organized you are, you won't get everything on your "to do" list completed. When this happens, transfer the outstanding tasks on to tomorrow's list before you go home. That way they won't get overlooked.

5. PRIORITIZE

We all know that there are days when you simply can't get through everything on your list, *and* get to all your meetings and appointments for the day, *and* complete major tasks such as preparing the visuals for Friday's presentation. That's where prioritizing comes in. You need to impose an order on the tasks, to ensure that those that remain undone at the end of the day are the ones that can wait anyway.

Importance

Begin by allocating each task a grade – "A", "B" or "C" – according to how important it is (see the information on Alan Lakein, Chapter 8). "A" tasks are the most important, and "C" the least important. Measure importance against the objectives for the job. If a task is necessary for you to achieve your goal of raising customer satisfaction, it rates an "A" grade. Organizing a leaving party for one of the team is a "C" task. That doesn't mean it doesn't need to be done – tasks that don't need to be done should never have made it on to the "to do" list; they should have been dumped before that stage – it just means it isn't as important as your "A" or "B" tasks.

Urgency

Before you can prioritize your workload for the day, you'll also need to establish urgency. Some things just *have* to be done today – like ordering training materials for next week's course, when the supplier needs five days advance warning for delivery. Other things may be crucial to the survival of the whole organization, but they can still wait a few days, or even weeks. Urgency has nothing to do with importance. Some of your "C" tasks may well be very urgent even though they're not really very important. Allocate each task a grade "1" or "2", where "1" is urgent and "2" is not urgent.

Order of priority

All your tasks are now graded according to both importance and urgency. So what order should you tackle them in? Here's the order of priority:

1 "A1"
2 "B1"
3 "C1"
4 "A2"
5 "B2"
6 "C2"

In other words, you should work through the urgent tasks in decreasing order of importance, and then work through the non-urgent tasks in the same way. Even the bottom tasks on the list, the "C2s", will eventually get done, if only because in the end they will become urgent, and jump up the list.

There is one point to add to all this: although you must do the urgent tasks first, you don't necessarily have to spend very long on them. "C1" tasks, in particular, should be done quickly or delegated; don't waste time on unimportant tasks, however urgent. Once you are in the swing of practicing good time management, you should find that you have many fewer urgent tasks in any case, since most of them will have been tackled before they become urgent.

By the way, if you find that you never get to the end of your tasks and the backlog constantly piles up, there's something wrong. You have got to cut down your workload or you will become stressed and ill (see *ExpressExec: Stress Management*) and your job won't get done effectively. If you are working as effectively as you can, using the best time management techniques, you should either:

» delegate more work;
» identify more tasks that can be dumped without detriment to you or the job; or
» talk to your boss about reducing your workload.

Staying late or taking work home with you on a regular basis are not smart options. No one should have more work than they can effectively do, if they are already getting the most out of their time. Some of us are in jobs where we occasionally work late for special projects, or rarely get away before 6pm. But staying at the office until 8 or 9pm most evenings, or working at home until close to bedtime, is stressful and demoralizing. No organization should demand it regularly of its people.

6. DELEGATE

Delegation is an essential management skill and, unless you are seriously understaffed, poor delegation is almost always the culprit if you have a permanent backlog of work. It is one of the keys to effective time management and, if you haven't yet mastered it, you need to learn to.

The thing about delegation is that it isn't just a way of offloading extra work. It performs a twin function: it not only frees up your time to work on the most important tasks, but it also gives your team members the opportunity to develop new skills. In this way, your entire team becomes more effective.

When you delegate, you have to delegate responsibility for the task. It's not simply a matter of telling someone else exactly what to do and how to do it. You need to tell them what to achieve, and then let them do it their own way. You'll have to specify the results you want in terms of:

» time;
» cost;
» quality; and
» any other constraints you need to set.

Then you need to get out of their way and let them get on with it. They will learn more, and get more satisfaction from doing it this way.

However, that is not to say that you should abdicate from the task altogether. You need to be available for the person to come to you with any problems or worries about the task you have delegated to them. The ultimate responsibility is still yours, and for major or long-term tasks you will have to give a thorough briefing (that's why you need to schedule time for it in your diary), answer any questions, and hold monitoring sessions to make sure the task is on track.

There are a number of key stages in delegating any task.

1 Identify the task and set an overall objective – your team member will need this to be clear about what they are supposed to achieve.
2 Decide who you want to delegate the task to – this will depend on the availability of team members, but also on their skills, their level of responsibility, and their interest in the tasks. Try to stretch people without setting them tasks that seem unattainable to them.

3 Set parameters – the budget, deadline, limits of their authority, available resources, and so on.

4 Check that they understand what you're asking of them – give people a chance to talk through the task and ask questions.

5 Back them up – even with limited time, you'll still need to be available to point them towards information they might need, clear the way for them with other departments, and so on.

6 Monitor – for long-term tasks hold regular sessions for the person to ask questions and for you to check that they're on track. Even for smaller tasks, informal feedback is important to make sure they're not struggling, or unwittingly heading in the wrong direction.

7 Evaluate – after the tasks has been finished, talk to the person about how they got on. For a brief, simple task, a few informal words will do. For a major task, a proper feedback session is called for.

7. LEARN TO SAY ''NO''

For some people, saying ''no'' is easy. Others, however, find it so difficult to refuse someone that they end up agreeing to take on work that they simply don't have time for. Some do this because they don't want to disappoint the other person, some take on certain tasks for the kudos, some want to be helpful, and some do it because they don't want to admit that they might have taken on too much.

Whatever the reason, you have to learn to stop agreeing to work you don't have time for (and that's time without working extra hours to get it done). There are plenty of ways to say ''no'' without causing offence, and most people don't mind being refused. They probably asked you because they know you always say ''yes''. Once they learn this isn't the case, you may be put upon a little less often.

If you find saying ''no'' difficult, try adding a positive note to your refusal. Always include some kind of compensating factor. For example:

» ''I'm afraid I don't have time, but you could ask Amanda – she's better than me at that kind of thing'' (obviously, don't dump this on someone else whose workload is as heavy as yours).

» ''I can't do it, but I can tell you where to get the information you need to do it yourself.''

» "I haven't got time right now, but I can do it after next week's conference."

All of these refusals sound positive and helpful, rather than negative and surly. Phrasing your refusals in this way will make it easier for you to say "no". Once you start saying "no" – or saying "yes", but not now" – you'll find that most people's responses are nothing like as dramatic as you expected. As often as not, they'll say something like, "Fair enough, I thought you'd be too busy. I'll ask Ali instead." You'll wonder why it took you so long to start saying "no".

8. AVOID INTERRUPTIONS

Interruptions are a major impediment to good time management. Quite apart from the time they occupy, they break your flow. You waste time stopping what you're doing and starting again after the interruption has passed. There are various techniques for preventing interruptions, but you must enforce them if you want them to work. Often, we are our own worst enemies. We ask our friends not to call us at work and then, when they do, instead of reminding them not to, we chat to them for 20 minutes. It's hardly surprising if they carry on calling us at work, in that case.

The following techniques will all work, but only if you stick to the rules as firmly as you want everyone else to, especially while they're all getting the hang of a new system.

» Shut the door. If you're in an open-plan office, have your assistant protect you from visitors, or use some other system – even a "Do not disturb" sign will do. If people learn that you're not to be interrupted, and you will not co-operate if they do get past the system, they'll soon fall in with your way of doing things. If you are interrupted, insist, "Not now; you can come and talk to me after 4.30."(Or whenever suits.) The corollary of this is that you must give people ample time when you do have an open door, otherwise they will have no option but to interrupt you. At least one, and ideally two, open-door periods during the day should suffice for all but the most urgent interruptions.

» When people do visit you, don't encourage them to sit down. They'll leave much sooner if they have to stand up throughout. If you have a second chair in the office, keep a pile of files on it, or store it behind the door, so it isn't easy for people to help themselves to a seat.

» If you can see the interruption coming, try to visit people in their office before they visit you in yours. This gives you greater control over the time; it's easier to leave than to ask someone else to leave.

» Don't answer the phone when you're concentrating on something else. Let your voicemail pick up, and collect your messages when you're ready.

» If your calls are taken by someone else, have them give out times when you can be reached directly by phone. It makes life easier if this is always the same time. This is why it's a good idea to have a system that you're always available – on the phone or face-to-face – at the same time each day, assuming you're in the office that day. The first and last half-hours of the day generally avoid clashing with other appointments or periods of heavy concentration for you.

» Ask friends and family not to call (or e-mail) you at work – and give them short shrift (albeit politely) when they do.

» Don't give out your mobile phone number too freely, or you'll never get a moment's peace. Ideally, have messages left at the office for you to pick up once or twice a day. Then the number can be given to just half a dozen or so key people. If you do give the number out, turn the phone off and leave messages to be picked up when it's convenient.

» Don't interrupt yourself. Learn to stick at the task you're doing, and not to keep stopping, for example, to make a phone call you've just thought of, or to pick up your e-mails. You certainly need breaks at times from long-winded or highly focused tasks, but these should be proper breaks away from your desk – having a quick coffee or getting five minutes fresh air – not ad hoc interruptions of your own devising.

9. MONITOR YOUR PROGRESS

You wrote down your goals in your diary or planner – so how are you getting on? If you don't look, you won't know. Check regularly to see how you're measuring up against your targets. If you're behind schedule, find out early enough to make time to catch up. If you're easily on target, see if you can't set yourself more challenging goals next time, and schedule in more time next month for those essential, objective-centered whole-day sessions.

Another area to monitor is how much time certain activities occupy. Now you're organizing your diary properly, you'll have scheduled in time for things like putting together next year's budget, or preparing material for a report. The first time you do this, you're quite likely to find that you allocated too little or too much time. Make a note in your diary or planner (where you can find it again) of how much time you actually spent on the task. Next time you do something similar, you'll have a guide to work to.

Some tasks, such as presentations, reports, proposals, preparing for interviews, and so on, can vary considerably in the time they take. Write down how long each task takes, every time you finish one. When you schedule the next one, you can assess which earlier report (or other task) was most similar, see how long that took, and allow the appropriate amount of time for it.

10. KEEP WORK AND HOME SEPARATE

Remember that the object of time management is not to get more done in the same long hours, but to keep your hours sensible and *still* get more done. If you have a partner, a family or any desire for a social life, use time management skills to get more out of your home life too.

In particular, set yourself sensible working hours and don't exceed them. Obviously, there will be rare occasions when a conference runs into the evening, or a project entails working late for a night or two up against the deadline. But keep these rare. Set yourself a target for the number of nights you will allow yourself to work beyond, say, 6pm – and aim to meet the lowest target you can.

And if you take work home with you, it doesn't count as leaving work early. If you can't get your job done without taking work home regularly, you haven't mastered the art of time management. It is only when you can work sensible hours, keep work out of your home life, and still meet your targets and impress senior management, that you can truly consider yourself an accomplished time manager.

KEY LEARNING POINTS

1 Clear your desk.
2 Set goals.
3 Plan your diary.
4 Keep a daily "to do" list.
5 Prioritize.
6 Delegate.
7 Learn to say "no".
8 Avoid interruptions.
9 Monitor your progress.
10 Keep work and home separate.

Frequently Asked Questions (FAQs)

Q1: Why is it so important to master time management skills?
A: See Chapter 1 for an introduction to time management.

Q2: What are the core techniques of time management?
A: See Chapter 2 for an explanation of what time management is.

Q3: When did the modern concept of time management originate?
A: See Chapter 3 for a description of the evolution of time management.

Q4: How do I prevent my computer from eating into my time with e-mails and time spent on the Internet?
A: See Chapter 4 for a perspective on the e-dimension of time management.

Q5: What can I do day-to-day to make more effective use of my time?
A: See Chapter 5 for ideas on time management for executives.

Q6: How do different nationalities regard time management?

A: See Chapter 6 for an analysis of various cultural differences.

Q7: What real-life examples are there of people or organizations learning to manage their time better?

A: See Chapter 7 to read about some time management success stories.

Q8: What is a matrix of prioritization?

A: See Chapter 8 for information on key concepts and thinkers.

Q9: Where can I learn more about time management?

A: See Chapter 9 for a list of resources.

Q10: What are the most important things I have to do to manage my time better?

A: See Chapter 10 to find out the 10 steps to making time management work.

Index